Group Exercises
for Addiction
Counseling

Group Exercises for Addiction Counseling

Geri Miller

WILEY

JOHN WILEY & SONS, INC.

Library of Congress Cataloging-in-Publication Data

Miller, Geraldine A., 1955–
    Group exercises for addiction counseling / Geri Miller.
        p. ; cm.
    Includes bibliographical references.
    ISBN 978-0-470-90395-7 (pbk.); 978-1-118-22122-8 (e-bk.);
978-1-118-22879-1 (e-bk.); 978-1-118-22890-6 (e-bk.)
    I. Title.
    [DNLM: 1. Substance-Related Disorders—therapy. 2. Behavior, Addictive—therapy.
3. Counseling—methods. 4. Psychotherapy, Group—methods. WM 270]
    616.860651—dc23

                                                          2011039261

This book is dedicated to Ron Hood, my husband and friend, who once again has been my steadfast partner through the writing of this book; to Gale, Abby, and Jason Miller, and Tom, Laura, Natalie, and Kate Prow—my family whom I treasure; to my personal counselors and fellow group members who years ago helped me learn how to live better in this world through their loving confrontation of me in a community of support; and to the clients I have had the honor of counseling in addiction groups.

Contents

Preface		*ix*
Acknowledgments		*xiii*
1 •	Introduction	I
	Personal Reflections	I
	Main Section Points	2
	Overview	3
2 •	Philosophy and Practice of Group Work	II
	Personal Reflections	II
	Philosophy of Group Therapy	13
	Types of Groups	14
	Stages of Group Development	23
	Stage 1	23
	Stage 2	25
	Stage 3	27
	Stage 4	28
	Group Leader Techniques	28
	Specific Issues	32
	Therapist Self-Care	35
	Words to the Wise	38
	Developing an Addictions Counseling Group	38
	Handling Stage 2 Confrontations of the Leader	41

		Addressing Specific Addiction Issues	42
		Developing Group Member Awareness	43
		References	45
3	♦	Group Exercises	47
		Icebreakers	49
		Addiction Recovery	58
		Family/Relationships/Culture	79
		Family	80
		Relationships	85
		Culture	87
		Feelings Exploration	88
		Group Community Building	96
		Self-Esteem	102
		Recovery Skills: Communication/ Mindfulness/Problem Solving	105
		Communication	105
		Mindfulness	106
		Problem Solving	107
		Values	109
		Openers	112
		Opening Statements	112
		General Opening Activities	112
		Specific Opening Activities	113
		Closers	115
		Closing Statements	115
		General Closing Activities	116
		Specific Closing Activities	117
4	♦	Resources	121
		Readings	121
		Workbooks/Exercises	122
		Icebreaker Exercises	126
		Websites	126

Preface

This workbook evolved from a dinner conversation with an experienced addictions counselor years ago who said, "This is a book [a workbook on group counseling] that needs to be written for addiction counselors." I remembered these words of Jane Albers, whom I respect and care for both personally and professionally. It felt like this book came full circle when she agreed to be a reviewer of it.

I have always drawn on my personal experiences, as a group member in group counseling, to remind me of the importance of a leader providing care, respect, and honesty to clients and creating an atmosphere in a group that is conducive to those factors. I was blessed to have those experiences as a client where group leaders and fellow group members helped me learn, in a supportive community, about my blind and hidden spots that were causing me problems in living.

Since I began working as a mental health professional in 1976, I have been involved in group work. As a counselor, I found it fascinating and powerful and have tried to incorporate it into every professional job I have had. In my Master's degree program I studied group work beyond classroom assignments, and my doctoral internship was in a counseling center that emphasized group counseling. Much of my counseling in the addictions field has been in group counseling. I have been privileged both personally and professionally to witness the healing power of groups in all of the settings in which I have worked, and specifically, I have seen miracles of change in the lives of addicts and their loved ones as a result of group counseling.

This workbook of techniques has evolved from trainings I have conducted since 1999 with experienced addiction counselors—each participant described one favorite group counseling technique. I have chosen specific exercises from this body of techniques and described them in a concise, almost recipe-like format for the reader. The goal of this book became to have tried-and-true exercises readily available for busy clinicians.

The book is divided into four sections, and the following is a brief summary of each section:

- **Section 1, Introduction**, provides an overview of the rationale of the workbook.
- **Section 2, Philosophy and Practice of Group Work**, is divided into two areas: an excerpt from my book, *Learning the Language of Addiction Counseling*, that provides my philosophy of group work with addicted clients and their loved ones; and four "Words to the Wise" sections that focus on core, critical areas of group counseling that are needed to encourage healing from addiction.

- **Section 3, Group Exercises**, provides specific techniques (separated into 10 categories) that can be used in group counseling: Icebreakers, Addiction Recovery, Family/Relationships/Culture, Feelings Exploration, Group Community Building, Self-Esteem, Recovery Skills: Communication/Mindfulness/Problem Solving, Values, Openers, and Closers.
- **Section 4, Resources**, lists readings, workbooks/exercises, icebreaker exercises, and websites.

Acknowledgments

I have had numerous excellent teachers in the counseling field who have been my mentors, supervisors, colleagues, and students. I am deeply grateful for the time and energy each one of you invested in teaching me about group counseling in the area of addictions. Through watching your practice of honesty, openness, and willingness, as you examined your strengths and weaknesses both personally and professionally, I learned and continue to learn how to be a better person in this world and how to be a part of the one human community to which we all belong.

I especially thank the addicted clients and their loved ones who I witnessed being brave in group counseling, daring to be different, and as a result, healing from and learning to live with the wounds of the storylines of their lives. Your courageous stories have taught me how to live and encouraged me to continue to believe in the amazing power of the human spirit and its capacity for change, especially in the context of a community of support. Your stories are the miracles I have witnessed that sustain me personally and professionally and are a wellspring of hope that I am able to pass on to others in my personal life and professional work.

I also want to thank my personal group counselors and fellow group members I crossed paths with years ago who helped me look at my blind and hidden spots as a human being and thereby invited me into a new way of living. Thank you for being a part of saving my life. We had quite an adventure together, and I am grateful to each of you for being my buddies on that journey.

I also want to thank the North Carolina Foundation for Alcohol and Drug Studies Board and its coordinator, Dr. Jim Edmundson, who invited me to be a trainer of group counseling skills, at their winter and summer schools, year after year. These opportunities allowed me to practice what I love (group counseling) with those I respect (addiction counselors), counselors who are working so hard to be a part of saving the lives of addicts and their loved ones who are suffering with the disease of addiction. A special thank you goes to Jane Albers, reviewer of this workbook, who currently serves on the board and kicked off the idea for this workbook over a dinner years ago.

Additionally, I want to thank the people at John Wiley & Sons, Inc., who helped me write this book in so many ways: Marquita Flemming, my editor, who has helped me be the best writer I could be on this book and on two previous books. Marquita's knowledge, precision, enthusiasm, high expectations, and sustaining support have been gifts to me; I'd also like to thank Sherry Wasserman, Senior Editorial Assistant. There are numerous other employees behind the scenes at Wiley who helped me, and I thank each of you. A special thank you goes to two individuals: Judi Knott in Marketing and Kim Nir in Production. Judi is amazingly bright, hard-working, kind, and thoughtful, continually dedicated to what is best for me, the book, and the readers of the book. Kim is thorough, precise, and delightful to work with on the seemingly endless details that go into producing a book.

I also need to thank my computer teacher, George Dennis, who remains kind, smart, patient, and honest; and Leila Weinstein, another friend and colleague, who assisted me in the compilation of materials required in the writing of this book.

I also thank my friends: Susie Greene, Kathleen Kasprick, Alice Krueger, Pat Mitchell Anderson, Laurie Percival Oates, Rod and Marilou Steinmetz, and Sue Sweeting, each of whom showed me kindness, compassion, and support in the safe havens they provided for me in the writing of this book. I also thank my Saturday-morning coffee-drinking buddies, who continue to believe in me personally and professionally.

I thank the employees of the Paul H. Broyhill Wellness Center: Jodi Cash (director), Paul Moore (assistant director), Michael Darling (personal trainer), and all the rest of my friends who work there and work out there for being one of the special, significant communities in my life who are a wellspring of hope and laughter to me.

Thank you also to the owners of the Higher Ground Coffee Shoppe in Boone, North Carolina, Matt and Gloria Scott, who let George and I work on the book for hours in their shop and for sharing their delightful personalities and intelligence with me.

And an extra-special thank you to Ron Hood, my husband and best friend, who read every word of every draft of this book and gave up weekend and evening time with me so I could work on the book. In so many ways, I truly could not have written this book without you. My thank you remains the same as it has been in other books I have written: "Thank you, Ron, for being with me on this life path. I love you."

1

Introduction

PERSONAL REFLECTIONS

This book, *Group Exercises for Addiction Counseling*, has a lot of meaning for me personally as well as professionally. I believe that group therapy, as practiced by experienced, trained counselors, saved my life—which is why I am writing a book about it. In group therapy, I learned, in the moment when I was engaging in specific behaviors, exactly which behaviors were inhibiting my ability to connect effectively with others and to set up a community of support with others. That is a nice way of saying counselors and fellow clients confronted me on destructive behavior when I was doing it, and I could hear, see, and feel the impact of that behavior on others through their confrontation of me. I hated group therapy because I lived in fear of it. I was terrified of learning about my blind spots and hidden spots and having them pointed out in front of others. However, I also felt cared about in group therapy. Counselors and other clients cared enough about me to tell me hard things—hard things for them to say, hard things for me to hear. People took risks to tell me things that I did not want to hear and cared enough about me to extend their own vulnerability as expressed in their honesty. They also nurtured me and supported me after the confrontation and reminded me that progress, not perfection, is important in living.

I learned a lot about myself in group therapy that has helped me immeasurably to live and work with others in the world. I came out of the experience knowing my flaws as well as my strengths. I believe it is easier for me to live in the world and, hopefully, easier for others to live with me after the experience of group therapy. That is why I believe in the importance of this workbook. My hope is that counselors can find in these tried-and-true group exercises ways to help their clients understand themselves better, thereby offering them more choices about how they can live their lives and break out of dysfunctional interaction patterns with others. My simple hope is that the techniques may be used by counselors to help their clients live better.

MAIN SECTION POINTS

1. Addiction is a significant problem.
2. Treatment of addiction requires a biopsychosocial perspective and a balance of grassroots-based assistance and research findings.

3. This book, *Group Exercises for Addiction Conseling*, is a complementary book to *Learning the Language of Addiction Counseling*, containing exercises used by experienced addiction counselors.

4. Group therapy is commonly used in addiction treatment because it offers interpersonal learning, a community of support, cost effectiveness, and a history of effectiveness with addicted clients and their loved ones.

5. Counselors are encouraged to adapt these exercises to their own practice.

OVERVIEW

The addiction problem in the United States has reached alarming significance. This widespread problem of addiction results in many clients having an active or historical problem with addiction themselves or having family members who have struggled with addiction. If clients have not had to address addiction in themselves or their family members, they often are aware of someone in their daily lives (e.g., boss, friend, neighbor) whose addiction problem impacts their life. Because many clients are impacted by addiction, all counselors need to have the skills to work effectively with addiction issues. Counselors who work primarily in mental health settings need to be prepared to work with the issues of addiction that these clients bring to counseling, as well as addiction counselors who work directly with addicted individuals and their significant others.

Currently, it is almost impossible to effectively treat addiction issues as an isolated problem because of intrapersonal, interpersonal, and societal issues intertwining with the addiction. Intrapersonally, the addiction may be in response to a trauma experienced before the onset of addiction (e.g., physical abuse, sexual abuse, dysfunctional family dynamics). Also, the addiction in the individual may be in response to some other interpersonal (e.g., domestic violence) or societal (e.g., homelessness) problem. Counseling, then, requires a biopsychosocial perspective, where the interaction of biological, psychological, and social factors in the individual and his or her significant others are examined. A biopsychosocial perspective can assist the counselor in addressing issues related to the maintenance of the addiction, thereby enhancing the effectiveness of treatment for the addiction.

Accurate, research-based knowledge of the dynamics of addiction is needed to provide effective addiction counseling. Currently, counselors may practice counseling on a continuum, where at one extreme is the grassroots (self-help) emphasis and at the other is the abstract research emphasis. In terms of the grassroots emphasis, the addiction counseling field essentially evolved out of a grassroots network that is still alive today through self-help groups based on abstinence. Because of this grassroots basis and a large body of self-help literature on addiction recovery, counselors may be exposed to myths about addiction that are not founded in any clinical research and then unknowingly apply such myths to their clinical practice. At the other extreme, counselors may be exposed to research findings on addiction but not know how to apply or integrate these findings into their clinical work.

These concerns regarding the training of counselors in the addictions field led to publishing my textbook with Wiley, *Learning the Language of Addiction Counseling* (3rd edition) in June 2010. This textbook is one of the few books attempting to find a balance between the grassroots emphasis and the abstract research emphasis, resulting in a research-based clinical application approach to addiction counseling. Counselors require practical guidelines and suggestions that stem from a theoretical and research-based knowledge base so that they do not inadvertently enable addicted individuals in an active addiction or enable their significant others to directly or indirectly facilitate the presence of the addiction. The third edition of *Learning the Language of Addiction Counseling* presents knowledge that is current, emerges from a biopsychosocial perspective, and is in a user-friendly, practical application format (case examples and exercises), facilitating the integration of knowledge into practice by counselors or counselors-in-training. The book, then, is being used by students and practitioners in the mental health field.

This book, *Group Exercises for Addiction Counseling*, is meant to complement *Learning the Language of Addiction Counseling* (3rd edition). In *Learning the Language of Addiction Counseling* (3rd edition), the fifth chapter of the book, "The Treatment Process for Addictions," has a section on group counseling that describes group types, stages of development, techniques, issues, and therapist self-care, as well as a case study and exercise. This section of the book is helpful to readers because it provides an overview of the basic concepts of group work and some group techniques (including nine group exercises provided at the end of the chapter). However, because the textbook does not focus on group techniques, there is limited information available to counselors on specific group techniques that have been helpful in working with addicted clients. A workbook was needed in addition to the textbook to assist counselors in treating addicted clients. The rationale for the workbook is as follows.

Group therapy is commonly used in addiction treatment centers in the United States. It is sometimes seen as the *preferred treatment approach* with addicted clients, because they can learn about themselves interpersonally through their interaction with other group members and learn how to set up a community of support, which is so critical for their addiction recovery. Also, group therapy is often used in treatment because of its *cost effectiveness*: More individuals can be treated in a short period of time by one or two therapists than is possible through individual work. This cost effectiveness is appealing to organizations that, because of mental health funding cuts in the current economic times, have the need to operate as efficiently as possible. Finally, addiction treatment has had a *historical record* of using group treatment in working with addicted clients and their loved ones because of both the effectiveness of the treatment and the community of support for recovery.

A workbook of group exercises specifically designed for the addicted population is needed for several reasons. First, many counselors are being asked to facilitate groups focused on addiction even though they may have limited experience in the field of addiction counseling. Second, many experienced addiction counselors are leaving the field as a result of retirement or in response to current budget cuts, thereby taking their clinical knowledge base with them and leaving neophyte counselors to work with limited mentoring in addiction counseling. Third, counselors are increasingly asked to hit the ground running, so they do not have time to develop group exercises of their own and additionally are often asked to run several treatment groups per week that require them to use different exercises in their groups.

The group exercises in this workbook are tried and true by counselors working in the field of addiction counseling. They have resulted from trainings I provided to experienced addiction group counselors at institutes held once or twice a year with 20 to 40 participants since 1999. During trainings, experienced practitioners described one *favorite* group counseling technique that they used with various addicted clients in terms of gender, ethnicity, age, and so on, depending on their clinical population. A few of these exercises were chosen for this book and rewritten to make them more useful for counselors working in various settings. This workbook is a collection of powerful exercises that can be adapted to a counselor's own practice. In addition, readers of this text are encouraged to shape these exercises in a manner that fits their population. Because the main concern of our work is the welfare of the client, counselors need to shift exercises to fit the needs of the group and the population being served. For example, homework assignments are not noted with the exercises because the counselor, setting, and/or group members may not be a good match for homework. However, the leader may choose to involve homework with an exercise.

This adaptability extends to the materials included in the exercises. The exercises in this workbook are primarily process exercises requiring minimal materials that are typically available in an office or practice (e.g., paper, pens). Any specific, unique materials (e.g., hula hoops) can be substituted with materials that are readily available (e.g., chairs). That is why this workbook does not have descriptions of materials required for the exercises, because counselors can change all of the materials needed for the exercise to meet the needs and interests of the population being served.

I wanted this workbook to be easily accessible for busy clinicians who simply want to pull something off the shelf in order to do something different in their next group session. Therefore, there are no sections on goals, objectives, conclusions, processing questions, stages of the group, and so on that one might find in other workbooks. When I buy workbooks on group counseling, I typically do not read those sections; instead, I immediately look at the exercises to determine if I can use them in a group context and carefully read those sections. I made a choice to keep the exercises short because I wanted the book to be user-friendly to busy clinicians who probably do not have time to read a lot about the group application but who want to use exercises that have been used effectively before with addicts/alcoholics and their family members/significant others. Nonetheless, in the second section of this workbook, I include some of my philosophy of group work, with general suggestions and cautions as related to the field of addiction counseling, in order to provide readers with a general framework on my perspective of group work.

Additionally, in each exercise I have fused methods and directions so that the workbook reads more like a recipe book. Metaphorically, then, the counselor is the cook: Explicit directions on how to boil water and the like are not being given, but the how-to on combining the components are provided. This workbook will not meet the need for group work training, although there is a general section describing my approach. I am assuming that readers have had training in group work, and these exercises serve to augment that training. Ideally, readers will have also had training in group work in the addictions field because of the unique flavor that disease brings to the application of group counseling. If readers do not have general training or addiction-specific training in group work, you are encouraged to obtain that training, because one can be an effective counselor in general, but it is very important to understand how group counseling operates so clients (as well as counselors) are not hurt in the powerful process of group counseling.

Group Exercises for Addiction Counseling is designed for prospective and practicing counselors who work with addicted individuals in a group setting. Several broad purposes guided the development of this book:

1. To provide addictions counseling group techniques to counselors in a language that is easy to understand and readily usable.
2. To provide addictions counseling group techniques to counselors in a format that is easy to access.

3. To assist in the treatment of addiction-related issues by providing tried-and-true group counseling techniques that address common issues counselors frequently need to address with their clients.

4. To encourage the use of techniques that enhance client awareness of addiction-related stressors and how to cope with those stressors.

5. To provide a basic group counseling workbook that can be used in many different addiction treatment settings.

There are 11 categories in Section 3 of the workbook: Icebreakers, Addiction Recovery, Family/Relationships/Culture, Feelings Exploration, Group Community Building, Self-Esteem, Recovery Skills: Communication/Mindfulness/Problem Solving , Values, Openers, and Closers. These categories were chosen because they are useful in group development (Icebreakers, Openers, Closers, and Handling Stage 2 Confrontations of the Leader) or because they are issues commonly faced by addicts/alcoholics (Addiction Recovery, Family/Relationships/Culture, Feelings Exploration, Group Community Building, Self-Esteem, Recovery Skills: Mindfulness/Communication, and Values).

I genuinely wish you the very best in this important work.

2

Philosophy and Practice of Group Work

PERSONAL REFLECTIONS

Readers may ask a legitimate question when initially being exposed to the addictions counseling field: Why is group work pushed so much? This question deserves a thoughtful, multifaceted answer. First, all human beings need to be in community with other human beings—although some of us need bigger communities than others. Second, because of this need for community, groups can harm us as well as heal us; group therapy is one place where we can heal from harm that has been done to us by others. Third, group therapy provides the opportunity to free ourselves from our patterns by offering chances to be and act different within a community of support. For example, there is a saying, "It is our feelings about feelings that get us in trouble" (e.g., our shame about being angry). This feeling experience is one that is common for addicted individuals and their loved ones. These group opportunities to be different within a community of support provide an exit from the "disease of isolation" that has been used to describe addiction. Fourth, storytelling by leaders and members is common in a group and, as a Native American elder once said, "Stories teach us how to live." Group members can hear others' stories of how they live with and recover from addiction because their defenses are down as they listen, and they can vicariously learn through others' stories. Finally, in this setting, the counselor is not a star, but rather models a healthy way of being in the world, draws out members, and encourages cohesiveness through sharing so a healing community can respond to the wounds of addicted people and their loved ones.

This section of the book is divided into two main areas. The first is an excerpt from my book, *Learning the Language of Addiction Counseling* (pp. 110–120), that focuses on group counseling. It is included in case readers do not have that book and would like to be familiar with my philosophy of group counseling with addicted individuals. It is also included because the second part of this section includes "Words to the Wise," a summary of group counseling that is based on this section of text, which has four areas: Developing an Addictions Counseling

Group, Handling Stage 2 Confrontations of the Leader, Addressing Specific Addiction Issues, and Developing Member Awareness. These areas were chosen because they are core, critical areas in the creation of group counseling that encourages healing from addiction.

PHILOSOPHY OF GROUP THERAPY

Group therapy is a common form of therapy used in chemical dependency treatment centers in the United States (Capuzzi & Gross, 1992), due to the roots of the addiction field in AA and the therapeutic community, both of which use substantial group work to help people change (Margolis & Zweben, 1998). Kinney (2003) reports that group therapy is sometimes viewed as a treatment of choice for addicted clients because of the power of groups and the ability for clients to learn about themselves by interacting with others, getting social support and feedback, and receiving hope for change. Vannicelli (1995) states that group therapy brings clients together who share the common problem of addiction, thereby helping clients stay vigilant about recovery. The author also points out that the popularity of group therapy may be in relation to its cost effectiveness. Furthermore, a common difficulty for addicted individuals is interpersonal problems (Capuzzi & Gross, 1992). For this reason, group therapy can be very healing for an addict's recovery process. As Yalom (1985) states, group therapy is a microcosm of the real world. Therefore, how an addict operates in the real world will show up in the group, allowing the addicted individual to work through those issues differently. Addiction is a disease of isolation; addiction is the solution to and the consequence of the addict's impaired ability to develop and maintain relationships. Therefore, group therapy is a potentially powerful healing oasis where addicted individuals can learn how to form and maintain relationships with others.

Because of the prevalence of group work, it is critical that addiction counselors have a basic understanding of group counseling approaches and techniques. This section discusses types of groups, group stages, leader techniques, specific issues, and therapist self-care. In addition, specific group exercises that can be used with addicted clients are provided.

Types of Groups

Corey (1995) discusses different types of counseling groups: educational, vocational, social, and personal. Addiction groups may be a combination of educational, social, and personal types. Also, some more structured groups focus on a theme of recovery from addiction. For example, Greanias and Siegel (2000) talk about ways to work with dual-diagnosis clients within a group context. Also, group work has been discussed from a Motivational Interviewing perspective (Ingersoll, Wagner, & Gharib, 2002). Some specific areas to examine in the creation of a group are as follows (Corey, 2004b):

1. Type
2. Population
3. Goals

4. Need
5. Rationale
6. Leader/co-leader
7. Screening and selection procedures
8. Pragmatics: number of members, location, length, open or closed
9. Topic and focus
10. Group norms (ground rules)

The leader of an addictions group needs to determine the goal for the group and then look at how to set up norms to encourage the achievement of that goal. These norms should be clearly stated in the pregroup interview. If possible, it is a good idea to interview individuals who are going to join the group before they attend their first session. A 15- to 20-minute interview can allow the leader time to educate the client about the purpose and norms of the group as well as allow the client to obtain a sense of the leader and the group. A balance between safety and risk needs to be discussed with each member. Yet, members need to be encouraged to "do life differently." This means that in the group they can experiment with other people on being different. For example, if the client is normally quiet, the client could work at talking more in the group. This encouragement may assist clients in breaking out of lifelong interactional patterns.

Some authors have specific suggestions for a pregroup interview. In this interview, the addiction professional can determine whether the client is appropriate for the group, hear the client's concerns/hopes, and provide group orientation (Margolis & Zweben, 1998). Vannicelli (1995) suggests that information may need to be given in this pregroup interview for clients who have been exposed to self-help groups without previous exposure to group therapy. These clients need to be educated about differences in the therapy group, such as stricter group norms on time and attendance, clearer boundaries, more accountability, cost, discussion of outside group contacts, discussion of group process, focus on and communication of feelings, and exploration of the past and present.

Many times, however, addiction counselors do not have the luxury of a pregroup interview. In these cases, it is helpful for the leader to make some type of contact with the individual either before or during the group, even if it is as simple as shaking the person's hand and introducing himself or herself. Even the smallest personal contact can facilitate trust with a new group member and help make the group feel comfortable for the client. If a new member joins a group without a pregroup interview, the other group members can educate that individual to the norms of the group as a part of the group process.

If the counselor does not have the luxury of determining group membership, this issue must be discussed within the work environment. A counselor may face having someone in the group who is very disruptive to the group process. This issue needs to be discussed with a supervisor to determine a policy for handling this difficulty. The counselor also needs to look at having reasonable expectations for himself or herself as group leader, the members, and group goals. If the counselor is expected to work with whomever is in the group without previous contact, the counselor may need to simply do the best possible work in the present moment of the group session.

A leader must be careful in setting the tone for the group. One of the important bases of a group is the norms that are established. For instance, the leader needs to make sure that people attend the group, and if they cannot, they must know that it is their responsibility to call the leader. It is helpful to ask members to attend the group five or six times to get a feel for the average group before deciding whether they like or dislike the group. Group members must know that they cannot be sexual with one another in the group because of how such a relationship would affect the dynamics of the group. They need to understand that if they do want to be involved with another group member, it is best to bring up the issue with the leader, who must then consider separating the individuals into different groups. Group members also need to be told the importance of confidentiality as well as the leader's limitations on enforcing such confidentiality. Margolis and Zweben (1998) provide an example of group rules and expectations (see Table 2.1).

Table 2.1 Group Rules and Expectations

Our groups are one of the most lively and powerful parts of our program, but to keep them working well, we ask certain commitments:

1. Come on time.
2. Do not come intoxicated.

(continued)

3. Notify your group leader if you will be absent or you know you will be late. Other group members are usually concerned about those missing.

4. Keep the identities of the members in strictest confidence. You can share anything you like about what you experience in the group, but not about others.

5. Be open to looking at yourself and your behavior and to giving and receiving feedback. It is especially important to discuss any alcohol or drug use in the group.

6. Although contact with other group members outside group can be beneficial, please do not become involved in any relationship outside group that would interfere with your ability to be honest and explore issues in the group. Romantic or sexual relationships with other group members [are] an obvious example but not the only type of relationship that can be an impediment.

7. A minimum of 3 months' participation is needed to learn to use the group, more to receive full benefits. Please give 1 month's notice if you plan to terminate your participation in the group.

8. There is a list of group members' names and telephone numbers because we think you are an important support system for one another. This list must be kept strictly confidential.

I give/do not give (circle one) permission to have my name on the group list given to members. (First names only on the list.)
I have read and agree to the above rules and guidelines:
Name: _____ Date: _____

(continued)

Source: *Treating Patients With Alcohol and Other Drug Problems: An Integrated Approach,* by R. D. Margolis and J. E. Zweben, 1998, Washington, DC: American Psychological Association. This form can be used or reproduced without permission from the publisher or the authors.

If a member leaves the group, the leader should allow the group and member a chance to say good-bye. If a member needs to leave the group and there is not a chance for the group to say good-bye, the leader may ask the member whether he or she wants a statement to be read to the group or, at the very least, allow the group a chance to acknowledge the absence of the member in the next session. It is also important to make sure that there are enough chairs in the group for everyone, including members who are not present. Even though it may sound odd to have empty chairs in the group for individuals who are not there, it communicates an important message to the group that members are still part of the group, even if they cannot make it to one session. For example, a leader may leave an empty chair in the group for a member who drops out of the group while the group discusses this member leaving the group and then remove the chair once the discussion is complete. This provides a ritual for acknowledging the presence and absence of group members.

Also, the leader needs to be aware of how different chairs in the group can contribute to group dynamics. If there is an extremely comfortable chair, group members may show "sibling rivalry" over that chair by coming early to group to obtain access to it, claiming it as "my chair," or quietly develop resentment toward another client who tends to occupy the chair. There is no need for all chairs to be the same, but if there are differences among the chairs, the group leader can use these differences to be aware of and comment about the group process metaphorically.

A leader needs to decide how to open and close sessions to see whether these actions will reinforce targeted behaviors. The counselor needs to find a way to open and close sessions that is comfortable for himself or herself and respectful to the group members. The counselor can choose the same types of opening and closing statements or different ones. The counselor may begin each week by saying "Let's go around the room and have each person say one word about how easy or difficult it has been for you to stay sober this week," and end the session by saying "Let's hear from each person, in one sentence, what you learned in group today about staying sober." It is important that the counselor make these choices consciously, because they set a tone for how clients enter and exit the group each session. Corey (2004b) provides some excellent suggestions for beginning and ending general group sessions that can easily be translated to addiction-specific groups. The use of exercises in the group also needs to be examined. Although exercises can be helpful in providing clients with a framework for the group (thereby reducing their anxiety), they may also reinforce dependency on the leader.

A counselor needs to find a balance between overusing and underusing exercises in a group.

The group leader also needs to examine how he or she owns power. This form(s) of power will hinge on factors such as the leader's theoretical framework, personal preference of a power form, job title, and client population. Seven possible forms of power the leader can choose from are as follows:

1. *Coercive*, which is based on *fear*. Failure to comply with the leader results in punishment for the members.

2. *Legitimate*, which is based on *leader position*. The leader has the right to expect that suggestions are followed by group members.

3. *Expert*, which is based on the leader possessing *expertise, skill, and knowledge*. The leader is respected for having these traits.

4. *Reward*, which is based on the leader's *ability to reward others*. The leader will provide positive incentives for client compliance.

5. *Referent*, which is based on the leader's *personality traits*. The leader is liked or admired for his or her personality.

6. *Information*, which is based on the leader's *access to valuable information*. The information the leader has is wanted or needed.

7. *Connection*, which is based on the leader's *connections with others who are influential or important in terms of the organization* (inside or outside of the organization). Group members want to have the positive aspect of the connections and avoid the negative aspects.

The first five forms of power are from French and Raven (1959), while the last two have been added in subsequent literature. The sixth one is from Raven and Kruglanski (1975), and the seventh one is from Hersey & Blanchard (1982). Leaders may have (a) more than one form of power they use with a group, (b) a favorite form of power, and/or (c) need to change the form of power they typically use because of the type of group they are conducting or the membership of the group. The leader must know and consciously use power for the welfare of the client(s) and for one's own self-care as a counselor.

Finally, if a counselor has a co-leader in the group, the dynamics of this relationship can have a powerful effect on the group. The communication between co-leaders must be very honest and open, with issues being addressed between them. If there are communication problems, they will be acted out in a group, just as marital problems in a family are acted out in the children's behavior. The co-leaders become parents in the group, because the group is a re-creation of the family of origin (Yalom, 1985). These projections will be strengthened if one co-leader is male and one is female. However, these projections can be present even if the co-leaders' genders are the same. One co-leader will typically be viewed as the stereotypic mother (caring, supportive, nurturing), and the other co-leader will typically be viewed as the stereotypic father (worldly, disciplinary). Leaders can use these projections to assist clients in healing from their family-of-origin issues, but they need to not let any difficulties between them as leaders be acted out with group members. The co-leaders need to discuss how they will deal with differences both inside and outside the group (e.g.,

How much do we tell the children about our marital problems and how do we tell them?).

Stages of Group Development

Different group theorists frame group development in various stages (Corey, 2004a, 1995; Yalom, 1985). The framework used in this chapter is Corey's (1995), which discusses four group stages: Initial Stage—Orientation and Exploration (Stage 1), Transition Stage—Dealing with Resistance (Stage 2), Working Stage—Cohesion and Productivity (Stage 3), and Final Stage—Consolidation and Termination (Stage 4). The counselor needs to remember that these group stages are not fixed or clear-cut.

Groups may show evidence of going back and forth between the stages, depending on membership changes in the group or issues that arise in the group. Also, when group membership changes for each session, the group leader may need to look at each session as one where each of these stages is touched on in that session. Thus, although there may not be a carryover from session to session in terms of group development, it primarily occurs each session because the group is so significantly changed in terms of membership each time. This perspective can reflect the approach advocated earlier, where the group leader has expectations that are reasonable given the context of the group.

Stage 1

The first stage of group development is what may be called the "cocktail party" stage, where members are nervous about attending the group. During this stage, members generally are involved in superficial chitchat that does not reveal much about themselves.

As Corey's (1995) title (Orientation and Exploration) implies, members are trying to orient themselves to the group and explore how they are expected to function within the group. A central issue for members is the theme of trust (Corey, 1995). As members are determining group rules and norms, they are also trying to determine a sense of whether they belong in this group and whether they will be accepted by the other group members as well as by the group leader.

Addiction clients may show these initial group development behaviors in specific ways. For example, superficial chitchat may be "junkie of the year " competition bragging. Here, a client may talk with other clients about how many different types of drugs he or she has used, how much of certain drugs has been taken, or how many consequences have been experienced (e.g., the number of DUIs). This information sharing may appear both deep and meaningful, but the client is truly sharing information that, to some degree, is already known by the counselor and other individuals in the client's life. This chitchat may serve as a distraction from the painful issues in the client's life that led to or resulted from the addiction. At the same time, this information is important for the client to share to determine how similar or dissimilar he or she is to other group members and to determine whether these members will be judgmental. The group leader, then, who should be aware of the need for such information to be shared by members, also needs to monitor whether this information sharing is an avoidance technique being used by the clients. If it appears to be an avoidance technique, the counselor will need to set limits on this type of sharing and encourage group members to share at a more personal level.

Stage 2

Stage 2 of group development is often a difficult stage for both clients and the leader. In this stage of group development, the leadership of the group is challenged. Prior to this stage, the leader may have looked like an omnipotent parent to members (Yalom, 1985). During Stage 2, members are questioning the leader's ability to direct the group. The members are really trying to find out how safe the group is for them. Knowledge of this level of safety emerges from struggles with power and control. Typically, this challenge is initially directed to the leader, in part to determine how the leader acts when stressed in situations. It is a parallel process to what a person may do in an intimate relationship to find out how safe he or she is with an individual by fighting with the individual or, staying with the family metaphor, how safe the kids are when the parent(s) is upset.

Once the leader has been challenged, group members will repeat this process with other group members. Group members will not confront one another until the leader is challenged because of the need to see how conflict is addressed in the group. These conflicts will show how the leader responds to conflict and how other members in the group act when they are challenged.

At this stage of development, addicted clients may challenge group leaders in a variety of ways. The leaders, if they are not recovering addicts, may be asked what they know about addiction and how they dare to work with addicts when they have never faced these issues. If leaders are recovering addicts, they may be challenged by being asked what types of drugs were done or how long they used. Leaders may also be challenged on gender or ethnicity differences, again questioning how well they can understand the struggles of the members. Vannicelli (1995) elaborates on specific challenges to leadership from a 12-step perspective. These challenges include the client's having an overzealousness of AA 12-step programs, being too literal about 12-step philosophy (e.g., "slogan resistance" in which the client uses slogans to avoid addressing personal issues, such as "live in the present" rather than address past issues), using 12-step program terminology in a defensive manner (e.g., "I just have to let go of it"), and using program labels to avoid experiencing conflict or differences (e.g., "alcoholic behavior"). Whatever the form of the challenge, leaders are questioned on their competence. This questioning process reflects the underlying anxiety of the group members and the level of resistance or willingness they have to discuss concerns at a deeper level. Group leaders, while responding to questions directed to them, also need to redirect the focus from themselves by refocusing the group's attention to the underlying anxiety and resistance and processing this anxiety and resistance with the group.

Addicted clients often have a poor history with conflict resolution. They frequently come from families or drug use experiences where conflict was "unchecked" and resulted in violence—physically, emotionally, or psychologically. The addiction counselor needs to keep this tendency in mind when working with addicted clients so that the group is a safe place where clients learn that conflict does not mean violence and that they can learn conflict resolution techniques. At this stage, the counselor can use conflict that occurs as a natural part of the group process to teach clients to handle conflict in a different manner. Counselors need to encourage clients to be aware and express their issues with conflict requiring the counselor to watch the verbal and nonverbal behavior of clients during group sessions. Thus, the counselor may need to encourage confrontation from clients to the leader so the counselor can be a role model for how to handle conflict and set norms for how conflict will be handled in this group.

Stage 3

In the working stage of group development, Stage 3, group cohesion has developed, and members trust and feel close to one another. Members share information about themselves on a deep and meaningful level. In the context of the group, they are now willing to look at issues with which they have struggled. Members are comfortable being direct and confrontational with one another. The leader is seen by group members in a more realistic light of having both strengths and weaknesses.

In working with addicts at this stage of group development, the leader may find that members are willing to discuss their personal issues in depth. Rather than simply discussing drugs they have used, they may be willing to discuss the shameful and embarrassing actions they took to obtain drugs. They may discuss how they felt as children growing up in alcoholic homes. Issues that emerge are discussed with an expression of vulnerability and openness. At this stage, members are willing to be supportive and share their own places of pain with others in the group.

Stage 4

In the final stage of group development, members are facing issues of termination and attempting to integrate their experiences in the group into their daily lives. Strong feelings about termination may emerge for members, as well as concerns about how well they may apply these group experiences to their lives. Themes of loss and grief may appear. The loss of loved ones through death or through the consequences of their drug use may be present. Feelings of abandonment and betrayal may also emerge. The leader, for example, might be accused of not really caring for the addicted individuals because the group will end and they will not be able to see the leader again.

Group Leader Techniques

Group leaders can facilitate the transitions in the stages of group development by acknowledging the need for certain factors to be present and by encouraging the presence of those factors in the group. Because two of Yalom's (1985) 11 therapeutic factors for group development—installation of hope and universality—seem especially related to the issues of addicted clients, they are discussed here.

Installation of hope is a very powerful tool in working with addicted clients. These individuals may have previously tried to address their addiction and found themselves back in it despite their best efforts. If a leader can communicate hope to clients, this hope may assist them in making important changes in their lives. The leader's belief in the client's ability to change may assist with the client's motivation level, as well as provide the client with support to make changes around addictive behavior. For example, the leader can simply encourage clients to "do it differently" in the context of the group—that is, to try different behaviors in an attempt to achieve and maintain sobriety.

This experience can lead to what Yalom (1985) calls the corrective emotional experience:

> The client heals from a previous trauma by re-experiencing the emotions in the group and having a chance to reflect on them. For example, a client may have let down many people in attempts to be sober and, as a result, has been ostracized from significant others because of the addictive behavior. If a client relapses in a group and has the experience to process feelings and thoughts about the relapse within an honest, caring, supportive group that holds the client responsible for the relapse behavior, the client may experience hope about staying sober. In addition, the client has the corrective emotional experience of still being

cared for and supported by the group to make another attempt at recovery.

Universality is the sense that the individual is not unique in his or her problems or situations (Yalom, 1985). This sense can reduce a feeling of social isolation for the addicted individual. One way for this sense to be encouraged is for the therapist to work in the here and now. In other words, the therapist is aware of what is happening in the group at the present moment and watches for items of similarity among members. Commenting on such similarities can assist with the sense of universality, which can provide a strong basis for the group to explore specific issues related to addictions because of the experiences they have in common. In addition, the experience of universality can be healing in and of itself because of the tendency for addicted individuals to be isolated from others as a result of their addiction and related behaviors. The universality can provide the addict with the sense of belonging to a community. For example, a client who has had extramarital affairs related to alcohol/drug use may have been isolated from his or her partner, children, church members, neighbors, and friends, who thought the affairs were a statement on what a bad person the addict is. Coming to a group and hearing how others made the mistake of having extramarital affairs may be healing for the addicted client and encouraging for him or her to discuss other issues related to dependency.

Leaders may find some other group techniques helpful when working with clients who are addicted. Connors, Donovan, and DiClemente (2001) state that while the history of substance abuse treatment has been confrontational in style in order to break the client's denial about substance abuse problems, such a style can result in client resistance or treatment dropouts. Rather, the authors advocate a supportive, empathic, client-centered style that invites clients to change. In general, group leaders need to listen actively; reflect meaningfully; facilitate goal achievement; and clarify, summarize, empathize, interpret, question, confront, support, diagnose, evaluate, and terminate appropriately within the group context. One technique that is helpful to group development is called *linking*. In this technique, the leader watches for ways to encourage interaction among the members by connecting the words and actions of one member to the concerns of another. This focus on common concerns among group members can facilitate the cohesion of the group (Corey & Corey, 1992).

Another technique is *blocking*, which is helpful in group development because the leader blocks member behaviors that work against group cohesion. At the same time, the leader does not attack the individual client demonstrating those behaviors in the group. Corey and Corey (1992) report some behaviors that need to be blocked: asking too many questions, gossiping, telling stories, invading privacy, and breaking confidences. For example, the leader can block too many questions by interrupting with a refraining comment such as, "It seems that the group members are wanting to know you better. What would you like us to know about you?"

Finally, group leaders need to use techniques that are a good match with the characteristics of the addicted clients with whom they work (Capuzzi & Gross, 1992). Leaders need to be directive by being focused and disciplined, which is important for addicted clients who may have low frustration tolerance and impulsiveness. They also need to confront both indirectly and directly to help clients break self-defeating patterns.

Leaders must also be tolerant toward emotionalism expressed by members and nondefensive, especially concerning anger and hostility. By being directive, respectfully confrontive, tolerant, and nondefensive, leaders can assist groups in becoming more cohesive as well as provide addicted clients with role-modeling behaviors that are helpful to their recovery process.

Specific Issues

When working with addicted individuals in a group, the leader needs to address relapse issues. For example, each leader needs to think about the conditions under which individuals who relapse will be allowed to remain in the group (Capuzzi & Gross, 1992).

There is a thin line between compassion for how difficult it is to change a habit and encouraging the addicted individual to continue using. Relapse is understandable if an individual has a commitment to sobriety and is willing to learn from the relapse by exploring it in the group therapy context, as well as possibly individually with the therapist (Miller, Kirkley, & Willis, 1995). It is important that group members accept consequences for their relapses. It is best that these consequences be clearly outlined in the group before the relapse occurs. For example, the counselor in the pregroup interview tells each recovering client that he or she is expected to remain sober, but if a relapse occurs, the client must let the counselor know of the relapse. This relapse would then be discussed openly in the group to determine what needs to be done differently to help the client stay sober. The client must understand that relapse does not automatically mean dismissal from the group (assuming the counselor is able to make such a promise), but that repeated relapses mean that the client's recovery is not working, and treatment alternatives may need to be explored with the counselor as well as the group.

Vannicelli (1995) also cautions group leaders about the issues of countertransference regarding substances. In particular, the author cautions counselors who are in recovery to (1) remember their role is different from a 12-step meeting, especially in terms of client welfare; (2) address the smell of alcohol in a group openly, even if uncertain as to who has been drinking; and (3) negotiate recovery contracts so they are supportive rather than automatic or formula based.

Typically, addicts have problems with authority figures, trusting others, emotional reactivity, and impulse control. Problems with authority figures are discussed in the section on therapist self-care. The other three themes, which need to be monitored throughout the group development stages, are discussed briefly here. Because trust of others may be a serious issue, the group leader needs to work hard at encouraging individuals to be both honest and respectful toward one another throughout the group sessions. An atmosphere of such honesty will assist members in trusting one another. At the same time, addicted members need to learn to work with their emotional reactivity and their poor impulse control. They must be encouraged to listen to their emotions and their impulses but to delay acting on them until they have seriously anticipated the consequences of their behavior. Thus, clients learn to recognize and express their emotions in ways that are honest and respectful toward others.

Two areas that may pose problems in a group with addicted individuals are denial and resistance (Capuzzi & Gross, 1992). Group members who have denial need to be confronted on the discrepancies of their behaviors, thoughts, and feelings. This does not have to be a highly emotional confrontation; in fact, a calm, neutral approach may help the client hear the confrontation less defensively, but the confrontation needs to be anchored in behavior. If possible, it is highly effective to have members confront one another on the presence of denial or resistance. Again, however, such confrontation, while honest, also needs to be respectful and caring. The counselor should note, however, that resistance in an addicted individual may be healthy in that the client may be aware that he or she lacks adequate support to address such issues. The client may not be willing to look at specific issues at that time because he or she does not have the necessary resources internally or externally to address them. In such a case, the counselor may encourage the client to state this limitation to the group and work with the client on building internal and external supports that would allow for such issues to be addressed.

Therapist Self-Care

One of the main areas that will assist a group in developing is this ability of the therapist to work with the group's transference on his or her leadership role (characteristics projected onto the leader). As Yalom (1985) states, the leader must remember that the transference is connected to the role. At the same time, the leader also needs to be aware that struggles with the leadership will be shaped by the traits/style of the leader.

These projections are examined in terms of group development stages and self-care practices of the leader. During the first stage of group development, the leader is closely watched by group members. When the leader enters the room, the members might become very quiet, and during discussions, members may turn often to the leader for feedback and suggestions. Group leaders will likely react differently to this focus of attention. For some, it may be uncomfortable to be under the magnifying glass of the group. These leaders may need to learn how to relax and be themselves when in the spotlight. Others who like to have the spotlight and be seen as having all the answers may need to proceed cautiously with feedback to members. In short, these leaders need to keep their egos in check for the sake of the group development and encourage members to be responsible for themselves.

The primary goal for the leader in the first stage of group development is to help the members feel comfortable in the group by making the group an inviting place for them to attend. The leader should allow members to have superficial conversations while also inviting them to look at deeper issues. The leader must closely monitor his or her own behavior, so the norms being set for the group are the ones the counselor wants to have set. During the second stage of group development, the leader encourages criticism from the group members. Here, the leader is monitoring for verbal and nonverbal signs of disagreement with the leadership. It is important for the leader to facilitate such challenges, so that the group members learn how to confront one another in the group and learn that they are safe even if they challenge the authority structure of the group.

The counselor knows that it is impossible to please all members of the group at this stage. Like the parent of an adolescent, whatever action he or she takes, the group members will find some fault with it. If the therapist is caring, the group members may say that they want more authority. If the counselor is authoritative, the group members may say that they want more flexibility. The group attack on the leadership will never be unanimous (Yalom, 1985), but to some degree, it will be personal.

The leader must acknowledge his or her flaws and possibly apologize to the group. The group will be closely watching the leader to see how he or she deals with being confronted. By remembering that the members are transferring their projections from previous experiences with authority figures, the leader will be less likely to be overwhelmed by the experience. It may also help to remember that allowing the group the process of challenging the leadership is exactly what will help the group move into the working stage. Thus, it is necessary for the counselor to learn how to take on the group's criticism. He or she must model an openness to feedback and find a way to ground himself or herself during the challenge.

This process of anchoring may vary among group leaders. Some may find it helpful to take a deep breath before responding to criticism. Others might place both feet on the floor and uncross their arms while doing a visualization that they are connected to the earth and that they will survive this confrontation. Whatever means of self-care is practiced by the leader, it is imperative that he or she not strike back at the group member(s) who is doing the challenging. He or she must realize that the individual is simply the mouthpiece of the challenge for the group—the one individual speaking is also speaking for others. The counselor, then, needs to encourage other members to speak their dissatisfaction with the leadership so that one individual does not monopolize the group and run the danger of becoming a scapegoat in the group.

Because many addicted clients have had negative experiences with authority figures, Stage 2 is critical in an addictions group. The leader needs to firmly guide the group through this stage of development by being honest, open, and willing to work through the challenge. Becoming resistive or defensive can stop the group at this stage of development.

During Stage 3 of group development, the leader turns over different leadership functions, such as beginning and ending the group, establishing the focus of the group session, or maintaining the physical aspects of the group space (e.g., chair arrangement, room temperature). This may be difficult for leaders who have a high need for control, but it is important for the group members, who have grown in their sense of autonomy.

During Stage 4 of group development, the leader must be comfortable with issues of death and loss. The leader needs to help members process their own grief reactions to the group ending as well as allow himself or herself a chance to grieve about the ending of the group. An important part of self-care as a leader is allowing yourself some supports in being a therapist. The feedback of trusted colleagues, a supervisor, or a mentor will assist in this area.

WORDS TO THE WISE

Developing an Addictions Counseling Group

1. Think of group development as **taking on a project**, such as building something, planting a garden, or cooking a meal. Do this even if you have limited choice about the creation of the group. Focus on those aspects of the group where you do have a choice. Once you have this perspective in mind, ask yourself questions about the type of group you want to create in terms of :

   a. Type
   b. Population
   c. Goals
   d. Need
   e. Rationale

    f. Leader/co-leader

    g. Screening and selection procedures

    h. Pragmatics: number of members, location, length, open vs. closed

    i. Topic and focus

    j. Group norms (ground rules)

2. **Know the stages of group development** in terms of your theoretical framework. Use that framework to guide your orientation in approaching each group session as well as techniques you choose to facilitate group development. I frame the development of a group as akin to life development stages: birth, teenage years, adult years, and death. This helps me generally remember what I can expect of a group at the stages and the kind of parent they need in a leader. At birth and in the early years, a parent needs to expend a lot of time and energy in the child's development taking on a primary caretaking role. In the teenage years, a parent needs to be prepared for challenge and to find a balance between encouraging autonomy and providing support. In the adult years, a parent needs to be available for guidance and support, but has more of a consulting role than a caretaking one. At a parent's death, the parent needs to encourage processing the loss for the child and encourage the child to embark on one's life without the parent. Thinking of group development within this framework can assist the counselor in the development of a group.

3. With regard to **exercise choice**, choose an exercise that matches the stage of group development of your group. Then remember four main guidelines. First, before using the exercise in the group, process its use with a supervisor, mentor, or colleague, have someone supervise your implementation of the exercise, and/or try it out on yourself first so you do not go in cold to the group with a new exercise. Second, when choosing an exercise to use in a group, multiply the time you anticipate by at least two so neither you nor group members feel rushed in the process; another exercise can always be added if there is time remaining in the group. Third, always have a backup exercise planned in the event that the one you introduce flops. Fourth, remember that group members can learn by watching others in the group (vicarious learning), so all group members do not need to process their experiences with an exercise at the same level.

4. Practice **leader self-care** throughout the group development stages. Be aware that, like a parent, some of us may shine as well as struggle with different development stages. For example, some parents may be exceptional with infants, whereas others do better in the child's adult years. As with parenting, leaders can learn both their strengths and weaknesses so as to enhance development as much as possible. The ongoing practice of self-care can assist the parent/leader in being the best he or she can be with the child/group.

Handling Stage 2 Confrontations of the Leader

1. In general, the leader can practice any of the following **overall approaches** to assist in handling the challenge in a calm, nonjudgmental manner that will facilitate the group evolution into Stage 3:

   * Breathe
   * Be calm
   * Intentionally slow yourself down
   * Own your power
   * Use positive, supportive self-talk
   * Have open, relaxed body language
   * Detach and look at the process: look for a learning opportunity for clients' learning skills, and talk about how conflict is dealt with in group
   * Don't take the challenge personally
   * Bring the confrontation into the open and examine it for underlying issues
   * Listen and be open (nonauthoritarian)
   * Listen to group member(s)
   * Reflect what the person is saying in the challenge
   * Ask the other group members what they think of the challenge
   * Check it out with the group if other people are experiencing the same reactions
   * Admit your mistake(s) and apologize if appropriate
   * Deal with the challenge by focusing on a solution and move on

- Help members be comfortable with nonresolution at times

2. The leader may also make **specific statements** that may assist in calming down both self and group members during this stressful time:

- "What makes you think that's true?"
- "Thank you for that information. You have taught me some things about myself, and I will take this into consideration."
- "Tell me more about your dissatisfaction with me as a leader."
- "What do other group members think of this challenge?"
- "What does this challenge remind you of, and how did you deal with it?"
- "What have you learned to do differently as you have challenged me as a leader or observed me being challenged?"

Addressing Specific Addiction Issues

1. Note that as a counselor, it is important to explore our own potential **countertransference issues** in working in the area of addictions counseling.
2. Be aware of **specific issues** that commonly arise in working with addicted clients, including:

- Relapse
- Authority

- Trust
- Emotional reactivity
- Poor impulse control
- Letting go (experiencing the powerlessness in living, including the past and loss)
- Denial
- Resistance

3. Choose **techniques** for the group that will assist clients with these common issues.

4. Be aware of how these different **issues may emerge uniquely** in the different stages as well as with different populations. Also note that members may vary on the amount and type of issue(s) with which they struggle.

Developing Group Member Awareness

1. Find out **members' beliefs about groups**. Ask what they have seen through different visual mediums (e.g., television, YouTube, movies) and what have they experienced as group members. Such experiences may predispose them to stereotypes about groups that are inaccurate, thereby inhibiting their capacity to learn about themselves and others in the group context.

2. Inform group members about what they can **expect in a counseling group** by providing them with a handout and/or discussion prior to the first group session or during it where they learn:

a. A definition of group therapy
b. Why group therapy works
c. What they can talk about in group therapy (including limits such as confidentiality)
d. How to participate in the group
e. The advantages of group therapy in comparison to individual therapy
f. The atmosphere of group therapy (norms of safety, respect, feedback)
g. Typical client concerns about group therapy

3. Stress that in group therapy they have the unique experience of learning about their "blind spots" and discussing their "hidden spots" through a supportive community. This information may encourage their interest and participation in the group.

REFERENCES

Capuzzi, D., & Gross, D. R. (1992). *Introduction to group counseling.* Denver, CO: Love.

Connors, G. J., Donovan, D. M., & DiClemente, C. C. (2001). *Substance abuse treatment and the stages of change.* New York, NY: Guilford Press.

Corey, G. (1995). *Theory and practice of group counseling* (4th ed.). Pacific Grove, CA: Brooks/Cole.

Corey, G. (2004a). *Theory and practice of group counseling* (6th ed.). Belmont, CA: Brooks/Cole.

Corey, G. (2004b). *Theory and practice of group counseling: Student manual* (6th ed.). Belmont, CA: Brooks/Cole.

Corey, G., & Corey, M. S. (1992). *Groups: Process and practice* (4th ed.). Pacific Grove, CA: Brooks/Cole.

French, J., & Raven, B. (1959). The basis of social power. In D. D. Cartwright (Ed.), *Studies on social power* (pp. 150–167). Ann Arbor: University of Michigan, Institute for Social Research.

Greanias, T., & Siegel, S. (2000). Dual diagnosis. In J. R. White & A. S. Freeman (Eds.), *Cognitive-behavioral group therapy for specific problems and populations* (pp. 149–173). Washington, DC: American Psychological Association.

Hersey, P., & Blanchard, K. (1982). *Management of organizational behavior: Utilizing human resources* (4th ed., p. 176). Englewood Cliffs, NJ: Prentice-Hall.

Ingersoll, K. S., Wagner, C. C., & Gharib, S. (2002). *Motivational groups for community substance abuse programs.* Richmond, VA: Mid-Atlantic ATTC.

Kinney, J. (2003). *Loosening the grip.* Boston, MA: McGraw-Hill.

Margolis, R. D., & Zweben, J. E. (1998). *Treating patients with alcohol and other drug problems: An integrated approach.* Washington, DC: American Psychological Association.

Miller, G., Kirkley, D., & Willis, M. (1995, January). *Blending two worlds: Supporting group functions within an addictions' framework.* Paper presented at the meeting of the Third National Conference of the Association for Specialists in Group Work, Athens, GA.

Raven, B. H., & Kruglanski, A. W. (1975). Conflict and power. In D. G. Single (Ed.), *The structure of conflict* (pp. 177–219). New York, NY: Academic Press.

Vannicelli, M. (1995). Group psychotherapy with substance abusers and family members. In A. M. Washton (Ed.), *Psychotherapy and substance abuse* (pp. 337–356). New York, NY: Guilford Press.

Yalom, I. D. (1985). *The theory and practice of group psychotherapy* (3rd ed.). New York, NY: Basic Books.

3

GROUP EXERCISES

With all exercises, counselors need to sensitively apply them to their population (e.g., regarding touch). Also, minimal materials are required for these exercises, and the materials are generally available in any office or practice (e.g., paper, pens). If some specific, unique materials are mentioned in an exercise (e.g., hula hoops), these materials can be substituted with items that are more readily accessible (e.g., chairs).

Counselors are encouraged to work flexibly with these exercises to fit the needs and interests of the population as well as the context and setting of the group. As with the sample described in the previous paragraph, a male prison population may not be open to using hula hoops, but they may be open to using chairs, and the setting may accommodate chairs more readily. Another example is with language used with the exercises. There are counselors in the addictions field who strongly believe that the phrase "drug of choice" is not appropriate, because individuals use a "drug of addiction/abuse," not one of choice. Counselors are encouraged to change the language of the exercises to fit their philosophical approach.

Specific time frames are also not provided, because most groups fluctuate in the length of time given the population and the setting; most groups run from 30 to 90 minutes. Exercises may run for a portion of the group time allowed or for the entire length of a group depending on both the leader's and members' interest and involvement with the exercise.

Leaders are encouraged to avoid providing a lot of instructions for the group exercises in order to encourage individual approaches to participation. For example, when asking group members to draw a picture of their addiction (Icebreaker Exercise), the provision of an example may limit the group members' drawings, whereas a general instruction to draw a picture will encourage members to draw on their own worldviews.

Some exercises might be enhanced with demonstration of the exercise before the group becomes involved. For example, in the addiction trial exercise (Addiction Recovery Exercise), the leader may want to make a statement proving that addiction is a disease followed by a statement that it is not and then pretend to be the judge and jury responding to those statements.

Note that homework assignments are not stated with the exercises. This is because the counselor may not have a setting and/or members conducive to homework. Many, if not all, exercises may have a homework component included if the leader so chooses.

The techniques are separated into the following areas: Icebreakers, Addiction Recovery, Family/Relationships/Culture, Feelings Exploration, Group Community Building, Self-Esteem, Recovery Skills: Communication/Mindfulness/Problem-Solving, Values, Openers, Closers.

ICEBREAKERS

These are exercises that help the group get to know each other or bond with each other.

- o Addiction Picture: Have the members draw a picture of their addiction and discuss them.

- o Favorite Meal: Have each participant describe the appetizer, the main course, and the drink they would have with their favorite meal. A lot of times this exercise brings up warm memories that the clients have of spending time with family and friends. The exercise gets everybody talking together about things that they like, and they discover a lot of commonalities among themselves. [Be aware that it has a tendency to make people hungry.]

- o Introductions (through accomplishments): Give the group members index cards and have them write down one or two things that they are proud of accomplishing in their lives. Have them exchange the cards and then introduce the person whose card they have. The person being introduced must stand up, and everybody should give them a cheer for whatever accomplishment that they've had.

○ Introductions (through other clients): Pair clients and have them get to know each other for about 5 or 10 minutes. Then bring them back into the big group and have them introduce each other to the group.

○ Introductions (through other clients—drug specific): Have clients introduce themselves to each other, talk about their drug of choice, and their expectations for treatment. Then bring them back into the big group and have them introduce each other to the group.

○ Introductions (through food): Have everybody say their first names and then add to that a food of some kind, such as "My name is Pat and I like pie."

○ Introductions (through hopes/dreams): Have each client share one hope/dream with the group. You may hear something like, "I hope I have a family one day" or "I hope that I stay clean" or "I hope that I'm stable."

o <u>Introductions (through leader):</u> Have a worksheet called "getting to know me" and have people fill it out and pass the finished sheets to the leader. Then, read them out loud without telling people whose profile is being read.

o <u>Introductions (through location):</u> Identify where individuals live in the state and have them talk a little bit about where they live and that type of thing.

o <u>Introductions (through their names):</u> Have group members write down their names along with an adjective that can describe them and that starts with the first letter of their last name. This helps the leader to gauge some of the clients' self-perspective—how they feel about themselves. Then have an open discussion about what each person wrote.

o <u>Introductions (through partner):</u> Separate the group members into pairs and have them introduce themselves to each other. Then bring them back together as a class, and have each one introduce his/her partner to the group.

o <u>Introductions (through self-facts):</u> In the beginning of a group, have group members move into smaller groups based on what they have in common. For example: Who was born in North Carolina? Who has a pet? Who is left-handed? Who plays a musical instrument or sings? Who has blue/brown eyes? Who has been to a foreign country?

o <u>Introduction (through topic):</u> The counselor identifies a recovery-related topic, which might be about relapse, parents, feelings (shame, guilt), etc. Whoever in the group relates to that topic starts a discussion about it.

o <u>Introductions (through trivia):</u> Give everyone a sheet of paper with five or six questions on it and then ask them to go around and find out who can answer those questions. For instance, if somebody was born in Boston, Massachusetts, then you have to go around the room and ask people if they were born in Boston or not. It's a way of getting people to know a little bit about each other.

o <u>Kindness:</u> Ask each member to describe an act of kindness they observed that day—without giving away any names.

o <u>Meditation Word/Meaning:</u> Read a meditation section out of a booklet and then have each member of the group give a word of the day or a meaning that they got out of the morning meditation and write that on the board. Follow this with five minutes of complete silence, and then open up the group and have each member tell the word they gave and what it means to them or how it affects them or what part it plays in their lives today. Then have feedback from other people as to what the word of the day meant to them in regards to the other person.

o <u>Motivational Change Quotes:</u> Have a group member pick a motivational quote about change out of the pot and read it, and then have the group as a whole discuss what that quote means to them, what they think that quote represents as far as recovery is concerned, and how it's significant to them and their recovery. Keep drawing quotes as needed to facilitate the discussion of change.

o <u>Myth or Truth?:</u> Gather around a table (as opposed to an open area with chairs, because of vulnerability). Let the group members select a topic such as relationships, communications, anger, substance abuse, feelings, etc. Then say "myth or truth" and make a statement. Allow them to tell what they think of or know about that topic. Put everything on the dry-erase board, and in the processing weed out what is true for this topic and what is not true for this topic.

o <u>Name Introduction:</u> Have the leader introduce themselves by name, for example, "My name is Andre." Then the person next to them must introduce themselves as well as the person who just went, such as, "My name is Kate, and that was Andre." The third person will introduce themselves as well as the two previous people, and so on until everyone has had a turn.

○ <u>Pass-the-Basket:</u> Put a number of recovery-related discussion topics on slips of paper and place them into a basket. Everybody gets to choose a slip of paper and talk about whatever the topic is.

○ <u>Personal Experience Disclosure:</u> Have one less hula hoop than the number of people in the group: If there are ten individuals, have nine hula hoops. Nine people take a hula hoop and stand in a circle. The person without the hula hoop stands in the middle and makes a statement about something he/she has done or something that has happened to him/her. If one of the people in the circle has experienced the same thing, they have to exchange places with the person in the middle (only one person makes the exchange). This can continue until all group members have been in the middle.

○ <u>Positive Statements:</u> Have each client go around and tell other group members something positive about them. It doesn't have to be anything related to friendship, just anything positive, such as "You have a nice shirt on," or "I like the way you've done your hair."

o <u>Question Cards:</u> Write down a bunch of questions on notecards (lots of questions on one card) and pass one out to each person. Have group members go through the questions and pick which ones they want to answer. The questions can include things like, "What was dinner like with your family? What was your last using experience? How are you feeling?"

o <u>Recovery Words:</u> Have group members write a word related to recovery on a piece of paper. Collect the papers in a hat (or whatever is available) and have members pull out a word from the hat and describe the word and what that word means to them. Another variation is to pick a word from recovery and concentrate on it and on how they can work it and make it a part of their lives.

o <u>Riddles:</u> Give group members wordplay riddles and form them into groups to figure out the answers, and then go over the answers with them.

o <u>Toilet Paper Sheets:</u> Have everyone take some toilet paper and then ask them to tell the group something about themselves for every sheet of toilet paper they have. Some people have a lot of toilet paper and some people only have a little bit. It usually gets a big laugh out of everybody.

o <u>Truth or Lie?:</u> Have group members (and the leader) tell two things that are true about themselves and then a whopper, which is a lie. The answers are put on the board, and the members have to guess what is true and what is not true.

o <u>"What If?":</u> Get everyone to write a "what-if" statement. It can be anything: "What if Albert Einstein was my father?" Then get everyone to pass their question to the person sitting on their right. The person sitting on their right then has to answer the question: "What if Albert Einstein was my dad? Then I wouldn't know how to tie my shoes"— something like that. After everybody answers, get them to pass their answers two spots down. Now everybody has the what-if question they were originally passed plus an answer to somebody else's question. Have them read their what-if question with the answer they have. For example, say someone was asked "What if Christmas was in July?" and their answer was, "We'd ride surfboards instead of sleds," and then they passed their answer to someone whose question was "What if Albert Einstein was my father?" they would end up with the following,

"What if Albert Einstein was my father? Then we'd ride surfboards instead of sleds." The combinations usually don't go together and that can make them really funny.

o   <u>Word Letters Missing</u>: Write a word on the board with letters missing and have the group try to guess what the word is. Try to relate that word to whatever topic the group will be working on that day.

Nonverbal Exercises:

* Have the group break into pairs, and have one person mirror the other's movement one-on-one with no touching.
* Have one person in the group do a pantomime. Another person should walk up to them and ask them what they are doing. The person doing the pantomime answers with something irrelevant to the pantomime. For example, they may be acting like they are driving a car, but when asked what they are doing, they might say, "Picking my nose." Then the person watching needs to create a pantomime based on that verbal response—they need to pick their nose. Continue this until everyone in the group has participated.
* Have one person lead the group in a nonverbal movement, with the others following. Then the group leader should name someone else in the group and have them

lead the group in a nonverbal movement. Continue until everyone in the group has participated.

- Have the group get into pairs, and have one person give the other person a shoulder rub, switching after five minutes. The exercise should be done in silence, with the understanding that no one is required to participate, and they can choose to stop the exercise at any point.

- Divide the group in half, and have one half of the group sit in a circle and act as the receiver. The other half of the group is on the outside as the giver. A person in the giver group touches the shoulder of a person in the receiver group for about 30 seconds. Then, the person being touched leaves the chair and the other person sits down.

ADDICTION RECOVERY

These are exercises that facilitate awareness of addiction recovery.

o <u>Addiction Goodbye Letter:</u> Have the group members write a letter to their drug. It can start off like they are writing a letter to a friend. Some might write three pages, some just a paragraph. Have them tell the drug everything they liked about it and what the drug took away from them and how it hurt them. Afterward, put a trashcan in the center of the circle and have each member read their letter out loud. After this, have them tear their letters up and throw them away. This exercise brings up different emotions, and it also provides a symbolic way of saying goodbye to the drug.

o Addiction Trial: Create two opposing teams out of the group, and one team has to prove that addiction is a disease and the other team has to prove that it is not. There is a judge and jury, and they go by the same protocol as in court.

o Balloons: Take into group five or six balloons of different colors. Ask one client what the most important thing is in his/her life and have the client take a balloon and toss that balloon from hand to hand. While doing this, distract the client from the balloon and challenge him/her: ask "Can you keep the balloon up with one foot in the air?", etc. Then, start throwing other balloons into the mix and have the client try to juggle those with the original balloon. The new balloons stand for other people or life areas that are important to the client. Use this as a starting point to talk about stress management in recovery and how to keep the most important things in our lives up in the air.

o Blindfold Experience 1: Pair clients up and have one of the clients blindfolded and the other acting as a seeing-eye dog. Have them tour the facility blindfolded: up the elevator, down the stairs, through the kitchen, bathroom, etc., along the way letting them touch, feel, and smell things. Using it as a life metaphor, after the experience, process in group how life is pretty much a blind journey that we stumble our way through, so we need to learn to trust someone under those circumstances. Generally, the clients feel helpless, confused, and lost during this exercise, and this is pretty much the state in which they come in for treatment. By having someone else help guide them through, hopefully it will establish some trust that they can depend on someone else other than themselves to help them find their way through life.

- ○ <u>Blindfold Experience 2</u>: Blindfold one group member and take him /her out of the group. Give each group member a piece of paper, and have them write down one obstacle in life. Then choose two people and take them away from the group. Explain to those two people that one of them will be a support system for the blindfolded person, and the other will be a barrier for the person. Then have the group members put their obstacles on the floor. Explain to the two people that they can hold onto the blindfolded person's arms, but they can't jerk them, they can only guide them in a direction. During this exercise, those two people will have to get the blindfolded person through these obstacles. What you want them to see is that this support person, or sponsor, is going to try to guide them through the right path—guide them so as to not step on these obstacles. The barrier person, who is going to be louder than the sponsor, is going to be pulling the person toward the obstacles and saying things like "Come this way, I won't steer you wrong, come this way, come on! Come on!" At the same time, the support person is saying, "No! Remember what happened to you last time? This is not a good road! Come this way!" They can use whatever words they want to persuade the blindfolded person. If the blindfolded person steps on an obstacle, they have relapsed, and they have to start over again. Do that a couple of times. Group members see a lot of struggle. When the group member makes it past the obstacles, stop the exercise and have everyone sit down and process what happened. Ask the person who was blindfolded, "What made you choose to decide who you trusted? Or, "How did you feel blindfolded?" It leads to a lot of conversation about how he/she made up his/her mind about who to listen to. At the end of the group, talk about what a good support system is, how you decide who you will trust, and how to make good choices.

○ <u>Board of Directors</u>: Start out by explaining what a board of directors is in case someone doesn't know (a group of people who have authority to make decisions about an organization). Then ask the clients to draw a rectangle and put three people on either side and two people at the head. Ask them to identify who is in what role: director, president, support people, etc. Through the process of talking about the people they chose and what their roles are, it might become clear to them that they might have to ask some of their "board members" to leave. Ask the clients, "Does someone need to ask somebody to leave the board? Are they supportive of your recovery?" This helps them to start thinking in terms of who they're going to ask for advice and who they might have to kick off the board and who to put on the board so they're more supportive of their recovery.

o   <u>Box of Stuff:</u> Start off with a box of random, nondangerous household items. Have group members pick one item from the box of stuff that they will use to describe who they are, where they are in their treatment, what they are there to work on, and what they want to work on in the future.

o   <u>Carnival Ride:</u> Have group members find a place in the room to stand and ask them to mimic a carnival or amusement park ride that represents their past experiences with addiction. Once they begin to do this, go around and ask them to describe what the ride is, how it relates to their historical experiences, and the feelings they have about that experience.

o <u>Client Story Disclosure:</u> Ask new clients to share their substance abuse history—from the first time they used up to how they have ended up in the group.

o <u>Disease Empty Chair:</u> Take two empty chairs and put them in the middle of the room. One chair stands for the disease and the other chair stands for the client. The client sits in the disease chair first and tries to entice the client chair to use again by telling the chair the benefits of using. Then have the client move and sit in the client chair and talk back to the disease. Have him/her discuss the consequences of using again and why they don't want to go back there. The exercise works well in breaking through the client's denial.

o <u>Disease Talking:</u> Have a client sit in a chair by him/herself and have other clients play the disease. The clients playing the disease should walk toward the client in the chair and entice them to use by telling them all the wonderful things about using and how fun it's going to be and so forth. As they get closer and closer to the client with more and more persuasive arguments, the client admits that he/she is crumbling. Then take another person from the group, who may represent the person's spouse, and that person stands next to the person and touches the person and starts talking back to the disease. The disease starts again at the back of the room and starts walking toward the client, persuasively giving the argument. Then as the person argues against the disease, keep adding support people (e.g., friends, group members, 12-step groups, sponsors), and as these people are added around the client sitting in the chair, the disease can't be heard over the din of the support people talking against the disease. Also, the disease can't find a way through the circle support which is all the way around this person—it can't get close to the recovering person. It really helps demonstrate how someone can't go it alone and the benefits of using other people in your life to help you stay clean.

o   <u>Dr. Frankenstein's Monster:</u> Create a monster—a drug- or alcohol-addicted monster based on the negative characteristics or attributes of a drug- and/ or alcohol-addicted person, such as a thief, a liar, poor hygiene, etc., as stated by group members. Then solicit from them positive attributes of a healthy, sober person: employed, honest, healthy, exerciser, etc. Discuss how they see themselves in their recovery based on these contrasting attributes.

o <u>Drug of Choice Obituary:</u> Have group members write an obituary for their drug of choice.

o <u>Favorite Song:</u> Have group members bring in a song that they feel is representative of them or of some aspect of their life—something that speaks to them. Ask them to write out the words at home and bring them in, and photocopy the words for everyone in the group. Ask them how they relate to different aspects of the song in terms of their addiction (active or recovery).

o <u>Graveyard Visit:</u> Have everyone write a letter of goodbye to addiction, and then take them to the graveyard and have the group members stand among the gravestones and read their letters.

o <u>Growing a New Life:</u> Give group members two illustrations of a tree—the tree should have a trunk, branches, and leaves. One illustration represents the life of addiction, and the other one represents the new life that they are aspiring to. In the illustration of the life of addiction, the branches are characteristics or character defects, and the leaves are the consequences or the results of these qualities and behavior. In the illustration of the new life, the branches are qualities the clients are trying to move toward, and the leaves are the fruits of these new qualities.

o Higher Power Jar: Use different kinds of jars so the participants can pick whichever jar they want, and hand out little strips of paper in all different colors. Instruct group members, "Whatever you want to give to your Higher Power, write it on the piece of paper and put it into the jar. Once a week, dump all of the papers out of their jar and read each one. If you are still holding onto what a particular paper says, put it back into the jar. If they are no longer worried about it or not holding onto it, throw it away.

o Hot Seat: Have the group form a circle and put a swivel chair in the center. A group member sits in the chair and acts as the client as everyone in the circle asks the client questions. After the client tells his/her story, have members ask a question of the client, and the leader throws a piece of candy to the member who asks the question.

o Issue Exploration: Ask clients to respond to the question, "What are you working on now in your recovery?; What do you feel like you need to work on?" on a sheet of paper. Have clients read their sheets aloud and allow discussion.

o Journals: Ask the clients where they would like to be in their recovery within the next year, and have them keep journals about that. At the end of each group, offer clients the opportunity to discuss what they wrote about (if they are willing to disclose that information).

o <u>Leader as Addiction:</u> In this exercise, the leader plays the role of an addiction. Group members write down 10 of their most valued people, places, or things in order of which is most important to them. Then the leader, as the addiction, goes around and takes away all of the valuable things (rip up what they wrote, say mean things, or step on what they wrote). Then, group members process how their addiction does the same thing to them, and they think about and discuss what kinds of things they need to do to prevent that.

o <u>Life Story Timeline:</u> Have each group member write their life story using a timeline, beginning with the year that they were born up until the present year, sharing and listing significant events that happened in their life. Give them specific examples to write down, like the first time they used, the first time they were arrested, the first time they dropped out of school, divorced, moved, had a death in the family—things that they can remember that stand out in their life. Have them write it down in their free time and bring it back to the group or sketch one out in group. Also have them add to the timeline what they would like to do from this point on.

o <u>Marble Transfer in PVC Pipes:</u> Put different sizes of PVC pipe into a bucket. Have each group member come up and get a piece of pipe and stand in a line leading up to the bucket. Give a marble to the person at the beginning of the line, farthest away from the bucket. The group has to work together, rolling the marble through the PVC pipes, to get the marble into the bucket. Eventually the marble drops and they have to start all over again. This exercise can be used to start a discussion about relapse, how it is not the end of the world, and about how they can develop tools to rely on other people and ask for help.

o <u>Me Bags:</u> Give the group members paper grocery bags and scissors, and have them cut out and paste things from magazines on the outside of the bags that they want people to see. Then have them cut out things they don't want people to see and place them on the inside of the bags. Then have them process through that exercise by pulling out items and explaining to the group what those are and how these hidden aspects of themselves impact their recovery.

o <u>Music:</u> Play a song(s) that is important to recovery and ask members how they relate to that song and how it speaks to them.

o Obituary Write-Up: Ask the clients to write their own obituaries. If they refuse (and often people do), say "If you continue your addiction, then you *are* writing your obituary, and the truth of who you really are is not going to be told." Sometimes they think about it and say "If I continue in this thing, I am going to die. Spiritually, I am dead already because I have taken my higher power out of everything that I've done in my life." It creates the opportunity for them to see things in a different light.

o Pillow as Addiction: Bring in a bunch of pillows, have everybody in the group pick one, and write on a board descriptions of the pillows: Are they soft? What do they symbolize? Why do we have them? How many do we have? Then ask the clients, "How many of these relate to when you were actively addicted? Was the drug something to comfort you that signified feeling relaxed, feeling peaceful?" Then each group member is told that that pillow now symbolizes their addiction for the day, and just like addiction, you can't put it down and you can't hide it. You try to mask it underneath things, but still everybody knows it's there. So the clients have to hold onto that pillow all day long. They can't put it down—even when using the bathroom. Then at the end of group, after five hours of having to hold onto the pillow, they are told they can now release the pillow (their addiction) and let it go and that it no longer has to be something they have to constantly carry around with them and bind themselves to. They get to keep the pillow as a symbol to remind them that you do carry these things around but you can put them down.

o <u>Post-Treatment Goals:</u> Have a group member identify a goal they would like to achieve when they get out of treatment. Have another member write the goal down on a piece of paper and stand at the opposite end of the room. Then, have the group member identify three obstacles that can keep them from reaching their goal, and have other members write these obstacles on pieces of paper and hold them up. Assign roles to the remaining group members, such as AA, therapy, couple's counseling, parenting classes, etc. Ask the original client to try to move towards his/her goal and have the group members who are holding the obstacles try to prevent him/her from moving toward his/her goal. The client must stop at each obstacle and consider how it would be best to handle that obstacle. He/she may also reach out to the other group members who are playing the roles such as AA. Continue until they have dealt with each one of the obstacles. This can help the client have a better understanding of how and who to ask for help when obstacles arise. Have a group discussion afterwards and let other members discuss things they have identified with.

o   Prison of Addiction: Show a picture of a person in jail with a caption that reads, "Why is this person in jail?" Then tape a caption over it that says, "What is it that keeps you in your own prison of addiction?" Have each group member process their reactions to this question.

o   Protective Wall Drawing: Have everyone draw on a piece of construction paper the walls that they put up to protect themselves from the outside world (money, sleeping, alcohol, drugs, etc.). Then have them explain what is on their piece of paper that they use for walls to protect them from the world.

o   Psychological Gardening Drawing: Have members draw a circle in the middle of a piece of paper and put their name in the circle. Around the circle they draw five flower petals. In each petal, they write one word across the bottom for the ground and then they draw a stem from the flower to the ground. Next, they draw four flowers. On the four flowers they put the names of the people, places, things, or ideas that are supportive to them. Below the ground they draw 10 roots, which are straight lines down. On the roots they write activities that they do or would like to do. Next, they draw two butterflies, which represent decisions that they made in the past that they are proud of. Finally, they draw four weeds that represent what will get in their way of doing the things that they like to do.

o Recovery Questions: Write down enough recovery-related questions for each group member, such as: "What is your biggest fear about staying sober?" and "Where do you see yourself in five years?" Have a group member pick a question from the pile and answer that question. After he/she answers that question, have the next person pick a question and answer it until all group members have had a chance to respond.

o Recovery Scaling Technique: Use scaling technique questions: "Is anyone here today doing any better in their recovery than they were yesterday? Rate that improvement on a scale from 1 to 10 (1 is the least you have improved in your recovery and 10 is the most). Comment on *how* you were able to make these improvements."

o Recovery Wall: Have the group members stand up and position themselves in relation to the wall in such a way that it signifies the degree of safety they feel about not relapsing: the closer they stand to the wall, the more danger they are in; the farther away from the wall, the safer they are. Have them talk about what that distance behind them means and what techniques they are using to give them confidence about that distance they are standing from the wall.

o <u>Relaxation Exercise:</u> Play a mellow type of listening music. Have participants lie in a prone position on the floor with their pillows and do about five minutes of relaxation techniques. Then tell them to imagine that they can go wherever they want with whomever they want. Use visualization of a pristine lake or a natural area (somewhere quiet and serene, a good place for them) and some sober activities they might do in that area. After that, come back together, and give them a chance to explain where that took them. This gives a lot of information about what things are comfortable for them and activities they like in their recovery.

o <u>Rocks in the Backpack:</u> Take rocks and write negative emotions on them, such as fear, hate, resentment, etc. Have the group members put the rocks into a backpack and have each carry the backpack around with him/her. After the group members have taken off and put down the backpack, ask them what it was like to let go of the backpack. This exercise demonstrates how we carry around feelings and don't let them go; it can lead into a discussion about the process of letting go.

o <u>Rubber Ball:</u> Hand a rubber band ball to a client and tell them to ask anyone in the group a treatment-related question. They ask the question and then throw the ball to the person who they want to answer. After that person answers, they then ask a question and throw the ball to another client.

o <u>Self-Care:</u> Ask the individual clients to do something good for themselves in their recovery and come back and discuss this experience in group.

o <u>Serenity Prayer Analysis:</u> Use this exercise when everybody is feeling overwhelmed and having trouble focusing on what they need to do in treatment. Draw a circle on the board and talk about the Serenity Prayer. Break it up and talk about the word "serenity" and "God grant me serenity to accept the things I cannot change." The outside of the circle stands for the "things I cannot change" and write all those things on the outside of the circle (e.g., someone's spouse's attitude about their addiction, whether or not the courts are going to take away their license, the past, etc.). Then talk about the fact that when we're saying the Serenity Prayer, we're asking for a Higher Power to give us peace over those things. The center of the circle

stands for "courage to change the things I can."
Here we write down the things we can change (e.g.,
I can share in group, I can go to a meeting, I can
come and sponsor, I can pray, I can do my assigned
work). This brings the focus back to their actions.
When people get overwhelmed, there tends to
be a focus on the outside of the circle, which are
the things we can't change. If they can do three
things inside the circle, it will help them get more
grounded and be in the here and now.

o <u>Sober Fun:</u> Discuss how to play and what the clients
are going to do with the hole in their lives that drugs
used to fill. Ask them to think way back into their
childhoods about what activities they enjoyed—
maybe about what they did with their father or an
uncle that was really fun for them. If they answer
with something like they went fishing with their
dad, suggest that maybe they take their kids fishing.
Also ask them to think of something that they had
always really wanted to do (no matter how silly or
not masculine) that they had never gotten around
to. Then explore resources in their community where
they could do this sort of thing.

o <u>"Spies":</u> During the last weekly group and just before
group is over, give everyone a piece of paper that
has "S-P-I-E-S" written down the side. This stands

for: Spiritual, Physical, Intellectual, Emotional, and Social. Each client has to fill in on the paper what they are going to do over the weekend (or the break) in order to be healthy in each particular area. For example, for "spiritual" they could say, "I'm going to attend a church service" or "I'm going to go for a sunrise walk on the beach." For "physical" they could say, "I'm going to work out; I'm going to do 20 sit-ups." Try to get them to be as specific as possible about what they're going to do. It's a way for them to think about the group even though they're not there and about what their goals are. During the following group, review each one's paper and what they did over the weekend.

o Stages of Change: Ask each group member what stage of change they are in (precontemplation, contemplation, preparation, action, maintenance, termination), have the person describe how they reached the decision that they were in that stage, and then ask the other members if they agree that the member is in that stage. Follow this process until every group member has an opportunity to share their perception of their stage of change and to receive feedback from other members.

o Using Versus Sober Obituaries: Get the group members to write out what their obituary might have been if they had died during their using days. Then have them write out an obituary from the point of view of where they hope to be after they have been in recovery for a period of time. Process the contrast between them in the group.

o Trashcan Activity: Sit in a circle and put a trashcan in the middle. Give the clients five pieces of paper stapled together and have them write down on each sheet of paper something important they will lose if they continue to use. On the first sheet of paper it may say something like "clothing" and the second one something like "food." Then you might have "house," "children," and eventually you get to "life"—the last one. Then, on the board write the statement, "If I continue to use *blank* and do not stop, I will lose *blank*." Go around the circle and have everyone repeat that statement and fill it in with whatever substance they were using, as well as whatever they will lose. Then have them rip off their first sheet of paper and throw it in the trashcan. Go around the circle again, repeating the exercise until they have thrown all of their pages away. It's interesting to see how the mood changes as the exercise progresses. At first it can be somewhat humorous, but when they start to throw family members (be sure to have clients use their family members' names), and eventually their lives, away, the atmosphere changes.

It is helpful to process what it would feel like to throw all those things away and to be able to say, "If I continue to do this, then this will be what happens."

o Using Names: Have group members write a street name that they used when they were using on a piece of paper, and then take that paper and burn it on an outside grill with the group standing around in a circle. The client has the opportunity to tell that name goodbye.

o Using Versus Recovering Descriptions: Ask group members to divide a sheet of paper in half and write "using" on one side and "recovering" on the other. Then ask them to write down as many characteristics about themselves as they can under these columns: how they are when they're using, or how people have told them they are when they're using, and then have them do the same for the recovery column. Ask each person to contribute one or two of the items they have written down under each category.

o Vacuum of Recovery: Have people make a list on paper of things they don't need in their lives anymore on half a sheet of paper. On the other half, have them write down what they would like to put in the space they have created within themselves by throwing away the things they didn't need anymore: What would they like to replace those things with? Then go outside and do a burning ritual where they set that piece of paper of things they don't need anymore on fire. Have them process in group their reactions to the burning and what they have left on their remaining sheet of paper.

o <u>Whole Person Wheel Drawing</u>: Have each client draw a circle and divide it into different parts, such as physical, mental, emotional, spiritual, etc. Group members can use the wheel to discuss the various aspects of themselves in their recovery process.

o <u>"Win, Lose, or Draw"</u>: Have a group member draw something on the board and have everybody guess the title of the picture, with the rule that the person doing the drawing can't talk. If someone says "bird," and "bird" is a part of the title, the person doing the drawing has to write it on the board. There can be different categories, such as movies, books, TV, as in charades. The exercise is useful for demonstrating that one can have fun when one is not high.

FAMILY/RELATIONSHIPS/CULTURE

These are exercises or role-playing games that explore family, relationship, and cultural dynamics.

Family

○ <u>Baby Book Therapy:</u> Ask parents to go home and review their child's baby books. In the following session, discuss their positive memories of the child.

○ <u>Family Constellation With the Victim:</u> Have the victim set up the scene with the perpetrator and have all the witnesses around and have the family constellation set up as the victim wants to set it up. Then, carefully go through the trauma situation as the person is willing to go through it. Focus first on the thinking, then the emotions and the person's feelings, and then have the person come up with beliefs about themselves. Ask them how they would like to change that belief about themselves, and have them write it on a card and then practice that card's changed belief outside of the group. Also, clearing is good for any kind of relationship where there's conflict or some kind of wounding going on. It can be a small process where the offended person says, "When you ____, I felt this, and it reminds me of _____"; possibly something from their childhood or memory. Then reframe that experience in a way that they would prefer. Have them tell the other person what they want that person to do differently, and tell themselves what they need to do differently. The whole group processes what happened and affirms the person who went through the experience.

o <u>Family Dinner Table:</u> Have group members draw their dinner tables and where everybody sits during dinnertime. This can lead to discussions about family dynamics, the importance of family and unity, isolation issues, etc.

o <u>Family Dynamics:</u> Have each client draw a diagram of how he or she remembers his or her family doing something, like being at dinner or the playground or a relative's house. Family can refer to a mother and father or to an aunt, siblings—whatever family is to that person. Afterward, go over the diagram and discuss what the client sees in the picture and what the leader sees in the picture. For example, the client may draw the siblings farther away from everyone else, or draw the mother smaller than the father, etc. This can lead to a discussion about family dynamics and also about connecting family dynamics from the past to the present.

o <u>Family Sculpture:</u> First, identify the different roles in an addicted family (e.g., addict/alcoholic, chief enabler, hero, scapegoat, lost child, mascot) and have group members volunteer to play the different roles in the family. The sculpture can be done a couple different ways: (1) do a generic family sculpture, where people represent the different roles and have them get used to their bodies and different props representing those roles, and then have a person act as an observer and go around and observe and/or ask questions of the people in the roles, or (2) ask for a volunteer to sculpt their own family of origin and then ask for volunteers to play the different roles in their family. Clients may not know what to do with the flood of emotions that the exercise can bring on, so for both options, have everyone sit down and process the activity after the sculpting.

○ <u>Family Treatment Progress:</u> Have group members write down and describe what their family is like at the beginning of treatment (What do we need to change? What do we do to achieve that?). Hold on to these comments. At the end of treatment, have them review that description again (What have we accomplished?).

○ <u>Grief Over Child's Usage:</u> Have parents bring in a baby picture of their adolescent and think about that picture. Usually this will get good thoughts going on in their heads, and then bring them back to why they are here (their child is in treatment). Have them look at the adolescent and ask them, "Did you ever envision being in this setting, at this time, with this problem?" Of course they generally answer, "No." As they're reflecting back on the picture, talk about each stage of grief and how it relates to their adolescent and their own personal feelings. It helps them understand where they are in the stages of grief and how all of those stages have affected them. It also helps them to understand that they are angry with this child for what they've done.

o Hollywood Movies: Use a movie (e.g., *When a Man Loves a Woman, Stuart Saves His Family*) and break it into three sections: (1) the building of addiction, (2) the treatment program, and (3) the recovery. Process the family dynamics operating in each section.

o Impact of Addiction on the Family: Have the group get into a circle while the family members stay on the outside of the circle. Ask the family members to listen, and have the group talk about how their active addiction affected their relationships with their family members. After they complete this, the family members get on the inside of the circle and the group members get on the outside of the circle, and the family members talk about how the addiction of their loved ones affected them. Then, have everyone get into a common circle and process. Some of the family members will have had no idea what some of their loved ones were going through, and the clients get to hear about some of the things they were doing to their family members.

○ <u>Mirroring</u>: One family member is the listener and one is the sender. They sit face-to-face and one tells the other something that it is difficult to talk about in very short phrases, short enough so the other person can remember what is said. The listener is to reflect back, as a mirror, saying, "I hear you say there's something you want me to talk to you about," and this continues as specifics are given on the listener's alcohol and drug use (e.g., "You know that time on Christmas Eve when you got drunk?" "That time on Christmas Eve when I got drunk."). It has to be structured very tightly, and the facilitator's job is to make sure that the person who is listening says back exactly what they hear, rather than what they have interpreted or understood, and that the sender is speaking in short enough phrases that the listener can repeat them. Each time after the sender says a phrase, the listener repeats it and says, "Is that right and is there more?" This continues until the sender has no more to say, and then the roles are reversed.

○ <u>Mock Funeral</u>: Do a role-play with group members playing the minister as well as members of the "deceased's" family of origin. Have them gather around the body and have the client (he or she shouldn't speak) observe his or her own funeral.

After the services are finished, everybody says their farewell, and the group can process the exercise to see what effect this has had on the client.

o **"The Jerry Springer Show":** Set up a talk show context with the leader as the talk show host who establishes the ground rules (e.g., no cursing, no chair-throwing), assigns roles, and recruits four volunteers (two parents and two children). One parent and one child is using and one parent and one child is not. The sober parent and child are "perfect," whereas the using parent and child repeatedly get into trouble. The leader gives specific instructions to each family member that will facilitate the dysfunction. For example, the "perfect" parent may be told: "Every time the other parent makes an excuse for using, I want you to cover for them because they make all the money for the family, so it is okay if they use." The rest of the group acts as the audience members, and they ask questions of the family members. After the role play, process the different roles that each member has played and how substance abuse affects the family.

Relationships

o **Desk Assistance:** Have the physically weakest person in the class stand on a desk. Then ask the strongest person to stand on the floor next to the desk. The person on the desk is supposed to help the person on the floor get onto the desk, and they are able to do this because they can work together. Then switch positions and ask them to repeat the exercise, but this time the person on the floor is told to not cooperate. This exercise demonstrates the fact that you need to be very careful about your own recovery when helping a friend with theirs.

○ <u>Impact of Addiction on Significant Other Visualization:</u> Have everyone close their eyes and think about one special person whom they love very much. Then have them open their eyes and talk in group about how this special person was specifically impacted by their addiction and how their chemical dependency has affected their relationship with that person. This helps them to see how their addiction became more important than the relationship with that person they loved and that that is how powerful disease is.

○ <u>Relationship Concern Index Cards:</u> Give group members an index card and tell them to write their name on it in large letters and decorate the cards. Then give them each a packet of small sticky notes and tell them to write on the notes the names of the people they are concerned about or fearful for, and have them put the sticky notes on their index cards. Then process what has happened to their cards. Often they will say things like, "I can't see myself anymore. I have an awful lot of sticky notes on here, an awful lot of people I worry about." This can lead into a discussion about what would happen if they let go of those people.

o <u>Significant Other Letter:</u> Tell each client to have a significant other write a letter to the client that expresses how the addiction affected the writer in 15 ways—have them give 15 specific examples of things they have done to hurt people as a result of their addiction. The letter is sealed and not read until the client's assigned time to share it in group. If a group member is adamant that he or she does not have anyone who can write them a letter, the group can answer or write a letter as they would imagine someone would have done.

Culture

o <u>Acculturation Process Assessment:</u> Tell them that the room is a map and tell them where Mexico is (and whatever other country is represented in the group) and where the United States is. Then tell them, "Go ahead and stand in this map where you were 10 years ago." Then say, "Go to the place in the map where you were five years ago." Then say, "Go stand where you have been in the last year." Then tell them, "Go and stand in the place where everything would be perfect and where you would love to live. Where is your heart, where is your passion?" and they all go back to that place. Lastly say, "Go stand in the place where the person you love the most, the person who is the most important to you, is right now," and they go back to that country. Process client reactions to the exercise.

o <u>Sharing Culture:</u> Have the group members get into a large circle in order to talk about what everyone wants to share with each other from their culture. The first person is given a ball of yarn, holds onto a piece of the yarn, and throws the ball to another person, saying, "This is my gift to you, I want to share this." Then that person holds a piece of the yarn and throws the ball to someone else and shares something. By the end of the exercise, the yarn is all used and it looks like a spider web. Have the group process the interconnectedness of people as well as our uniqueness.

FEELINGS EXPLORATION

These are exercises that help clients identify feelings.

o <u>Body Awareness 1</u>: If a client has a feeling that they cannot name, it can be helpful to ask him/her where the feeling is in his/her body. If he/she answers, "It's like a fist in my throat," or "It's like a ball in my stomach," you can ask him to describe it: what it feels like, looks like, what is its shape and size. Once the client begins to talk about what the problem is in terms of his/her body, you can work together on it through imagery. For example, if a client says her heart is as cold as ice, ask, "Would you like to get it warmer? Would you like to change it?" and if so, ask, "How would you want to warm up your heart?" The client may respond, "I guess I put a blanket around it," and the counselor can say, "Well, then get a blanket and put it around your heart." Then process the thoughts and feelings with the experience.

o <u>Body Awareness 2</u>: Ask everybody to freeze their facial expression and body language and then answer the question, "What would your facial expression say if it could talk for you?" They may say things like, "If my facial expression could talk it would say, 'I'm really annoyed with that person over there,'" or, "I really don't want to be in group today," or, "I'm really hopeful that we can talk about this or that."

o <u>Cognitive-Behavioral Triangle</u>: Have clients talk about behaviors they have engaged in or feelings they have had, and they can use the triangle to connect their behavior to their feelings and their thoughts. This can help illustrate that behavior can change based on what one is feeling, and that if feelings and thoughts are changed, behavior can also be changed.

o Discussion of Fear: Give each client three pieces of paper. Ask them to write on each piece of paper what their fears are. After they write one fear on each piece, they crumple up each piece of paper into a snowball. Then they all have to throw their snowballs at each other on the count of three. They can throw them at anybody, but they cannot throw all three of their papers at the same person. Everybody has to pick up the snowball closest to them and then go around the room and read the fear that someone else wrote about. Encourage them to talk about whether they identify with that fear and whether they can identify who the fear belonged to.

o Emotional Description: Get a person to describe what emotion they're feeling at the moment and talk about that. Ask the group to respond about what emotions they feel as the other person is talking. Draw commonality among the members by talking about what everyone is feeling at that time.

o <u>Emotional Disclosure ("A Matter of Concern")</u>:
   Have everybody write their name on the top of a
   sheet of paper followed by a matter of emotional
   concern. It can be very brief: "I'm angry at my wife."
   "I'm sad because my dog died." Have them turn the
   paper into the counselor. Then have some group
   members choose other group members to act as their
   counselors. The "client" group member will tell the
   "counselor" group member what is going on, and the
   "counselor" will give them feedback, so there is a one-
   on-one inside the group.

o <u>Feelings Bowl:</u> Take a bowl with feelings words
   written on paper in it and have each group member
   draw one out. Then have them each describe a scene
   that comes to their minds when they think of the
   word and how it relates to their lives.

o <u>Feelings Cards:</u> Write down various feelings on index
   cards (e.g., anger, guilt, loneliness), and then pass out
   the cards to various members and have them share
   experiences related to their childhood, teen years, and
   adult years that connect to the feelings card they draw.

o <u>Feelings Chart:</u> Use a large, colorful feeling and
   emotion words chart (or draw one on a board). Have
   a client pick one of the feelings or emotions that he/
   she is experiencing that day and process it. Then have

the other group members discuss how they feel in response to what the client said.

o <u>Half Smile:</u> Ask each member of the group to identify a person that they really, really dislike or hate. Then ask the members to close their eyes, put a half smile on their face, and continue to smile throughout the whole episode. Then ask them, while they have their eyes closed and they're smiling, to picture the person they dislike and to think about what it is they hate most about them. Then ask, "What is it like to be this person? What do you think motivates them to act the way they do?" as well as any other improvised questions. Lastly, ask them to think about how they envision this person now. Then all of the members open their eyes and the group processes each member's reaction to the exercise.

o <u>Human Being Pillow:</u> Take a pillow and tell the group to imagine that the words "I am a human being" are written on the pillow. Toss the pillow to one of the more talkative group members and ask them to share something they feel. When they are done, have them toss the pillow to someone else and say, "Remember, you are a human being too."

o <u>"I Take Responsibility":</u> Have each group member state the emotion that they have at that time and state that they take responsibility for it. For example, "I'm angry today and I take responsibility for it."

o Leader Pose: The leader asks everybody to close their eyes and then strikes a pose. When they open their eyes, they look at the leader (e.g., standing on a chair, crossing arms, staring down at them, etc.) and process how they feel: Does it remind them of any person or experience from their past?

o Military Metaphor: Ask members to use the different branches of service to describe how they are feeling.

o Object Projection: If someone is having trouble expressing their feelings, it can be useful to give them some sort of inanimate object, such as a ball or a pen, and have them project themselves onto that object and describe what the pen or the ball is feeling. This helps them to describe their feelings indirectly.

o "Shoulds": Have the clients write down "shoulds" on a sheet of paper, such as, "I should be married, because I'm 40 years old," or "I should have a family," and then have them write down as many shoulds as they feel comfortable letting go of. They have to write them down on a small piece of paper, and then tape them to helium-filled balloons that are taken outside.

Ask them, "Are you ready to let go of this thing that's holding you back?" and if they are ready, tell them they can release their balloon. If they're not, then they have to hold onto it.

o <u>T-Shirt/Sweatshirt:</u> Have group members draw a T-shirt or undershirt on a piece of paper. On that shirt have them write feelings about things that they have done that they don't want anyone to know about. Then on a separate sheet of paper, have them draw a sweatshirt that represents what they want to project to the world. This exercise helps them talk about feelings more and explore the two different "shirts."

o <u>The Supermarket:</u> Have the group members imagine that they are in a supermarket. They are to pick up an item they would like to be, bring it back, and put it inside the bag. The room symbolizes the bag: the floor is the bottom and the ceiling is the top. The members then imagine themselves to be the item and they place themselves in the bag. Ask them what they are in the bag and why they choose to be that item. If someone says that they are a loaf of bread and there is a ham sitting on top of him/her, ask him/her how he/she feels about that. If somebody picks a dozen eggs it might signal that he/she is feeling fragile. If someone picks a six-pack of Coke and sets him/herself in the bottom of the bag it may signal that he/she feels that he/she is carrying all of the weight.

o <u>Toys/Stuffed Animals:</u> Have clients pick a toy or stuffed animal that describes how they feel that day as they enter the room. They then explain why they feel like that animal today.

o <u>Traffic Jam:</u> Take seven carpet squares and line them up in a row. Get six volunteers and have them all line up facing each other, three on one side and three on the other side with an empty carpet square in the middle. The object for participants 1, 2, and 3 is to replace participants 4, 5, and 6, who are facing them. The only way they can do this is to move forward in front of someone standing in front of them. They can only move onto an empty square if it is in front of them. They can't move back. Allow them to decide how to do it. They go back and forth intertwining and they jam themselves up. They get to the point that they can't move anymore, and they have to go back and start over. They may start over three, four, or 15 times before they actually get it. Ask them at the end to describe the thoughts and feelings that came into their minds as they went through the exercise. Write down the thoughts and feelings on the board. Then, ask them to shift gears and reflect back to their acts of addiction and remember similar thoughts and feelings that they had in their active addiction and to write those feelings down. Then go back to discussing the carpet exercise and ask them how they felt once the process was completed and they had had some measure of success. Ask them what their definition of success is and how it makes them feel and how they are successful in their recovery.

o Underline: Water Bowl: Take a bowl of water and put it in the middle of the room. Give each client a cup to dip into the water, not knowing what they are going to do with it. Stand in a circle around the water and go around the room, starting with the leader, and say, "What I'm thirsting for today is _____." Have them fill the blank with the first thing that comes to their minds.

GROUP COMMUNITY BUILDING

These are exercises that help promote group cohesion and/or help group members discover that they have things in common with each other.

o Communication Building: Take a piece of construction paper and cut it into a puzzle. Divide the group into two or three smaller groups, and give each group their own puzzle. Give two or three puzzle pieces to each group's members. They are not allowed to talk to each other, and there can be no leader in the group. They have to put this puzzle together with nonverbal communication. It will sometimes take them 15 to 30 minutes to do this, because they are not allowed to grab puzzle pieces from each other, there is absolutely no talking, pointing, or stretching, and they have to work together as a team. At the end of it, talk about how frustrating it is not to be able to talk to each other and how difficult it is to have to rely on each other and depend on each other when nobody is listening. Talk about how in group when we have a breakdown in communication it makes the group ineffective because you can't accomplish anything that you need to get done.

o Courtroom: When new clients come into group, have it set up like a courtroom: the experienced group members are the jury, district attorney, and defense attorney (representing the new client), and the leader is the judge. Each new client introduces oneself, one's drug of choice, number of treatments, and how seriously he or she is taking treatment. The jury, district attorney, and judge all pretend to get to decide whether or not the new client can come into the group and decide what issues need to be addressed. While the leader makes the final decision, everybody has input, and the group works together collaboratively. The exercise helps create a cohesiveness and unity within the group and helps everybody get to know each other.

o <u>Criminal Issues:</u> Ask what criminal issues group members are struggling with at that time, discuss them, and process feedback they receive from their peers.

o <u>Emotional Bonding:</u> Have group members introduce themselves on a first-name basis and share a little bit about themselves. Have them share a feeling and emotion that they are experiencing at that time. After that brief introduction, ask the group to point out the members they are most concerned about.

o <u>Group as a Mirror:</u> After the group has been going awhile, have some of the group members sit in a circle and have the rest of the group members sit outside of the circle. Then conduct 45 to 50 minutes of group with the members in the circle and let the members sitting outside the circle observe. This can act as a healing exercise and can also help the observers identify with things that they may not have in previous groups.

o <u>Group Member Evaluation:</u> Have group members who know each other well evaluate each other about how they are doing in their recovery as well as with their mental illness, if that is a factor. Sometimes this creates a lot of positive interaction, although occasionally it creates confrontation.

o   <u>Hula Hoop Balance:</u> Group members stand in a circle where each member holds out one of their fingers and a hula hoop is placed on the group members' fingers. They begin by holding the hoop at a certain level and then bringing it down to the floor and then back up again without the hoop falling. This exercise can be done in silence or with group members talking with one another. Then process the group members' reactions to the experience.

o   <u>Hula Hoop Pass:</u> Have members form a circle where one member holds onto a hula hoop with one hand. Members then pass the hula hoop to one another, but they continue to hold the hula hoop until all members are holding it. Then process the experience with the group.

o   <u>Leader Modeling:</u> Turn the group over to one of the group members. The member of the group who is leading tries to emulate the leader as a counselor.

o   <u>Mapping the Past Drawing:</u> Everyone is given a large piece of paper, they draw whatever they want to draw on it, and they map out their life from as early as they can remember to the current date of any important experiences they've had—anything that has either positively or negatively impacted them. After everyone finishes, go over the maps and look for patterns in their experiences and how these have affected their present life.

o   <u>Musical Chairs:</u> Play musical chairs for about 30 minutes and then process what the group members have seen in each other. Group members tend to show childhood behaviors.

o   <u>Nonmusical Chairs:</u> Have one chair less in the group than the number of group members. Ask group members to sit down, and the person left standing goes to the middle of the circle and says something personal about themselves and then states something like, "Anyone who has a name starting with an A come to the middle." That person exchanges places with the person in the middle. This continues until everyone in the group has the opportunity to be in the middle and share personal information.

o   <u>Positive Feedback:</u> Have clients write their names on a piece of paper and then tape the papers to the back of each client. Have each client write one positive strength that they see in that individual on the piece of paper; have them do this for each group member. Stress that everybody has a positive strength that they can deal with.

o   <u>Ropes Course:</u> Take clients to a ropes course and challenge them on different activities. Even though most of the clients have experienced tragic and negative consequences as a result of their drug use, they have also become comfortable with those consequences, and they are afraid to get out of their comfort zones. The ropes course activities are designed to get them out of that comfort zone and also to create bonding, because a lot of the activities cannot be successfully accomplished without touching and without communicating with each other.

o   <u>Santa:</u> Use a small stuffed teddy bear called "Santa," and do not let group members talk until they have Santa in their hands. If they would like to talk, then they have to raise their hand in order to get Santa. If someone has Santa and somebody else wants him, the person who has him can hold onto him until they have finished what they have to say.

o   <u>Stereotype Line:</u> Ask for five volunteers and arrange them in a line. Pick one member out of the group and have them organize everybody according to their age—from youngest to oldest—and plug themselves in where they think they belong. They cannot ask the people their age. Have each person try to do this. Afterward, find out who was right (or most right). Then discuss how we cannot judge a book by its cover.

SELF-ESTEEM

These are exercises that help clients work on their self-esteem.

- ○ <u>Admired People:</u> Ask the group members to name three to five people that they admire and put down two adjectives that describe why they admire those people. Process the experience by focusing on the clients' description of these people reflecting who they are as people. An additional component is to have them circle the adjectives that are the same or similar, thereby reflecting the client's values.

- ○ <u>Compliment Exchange:</u> Have a group member turn to the person to their left and give that person a compliment. Have each member do this in turn until everyone in the group has received a compliment. Then have a group member start the same process with the person to their right until everybody in this direction has received a compliment. Afterward, the group processes and discusses whether they had difficulty giving or receiving a compliment.

o Group Member Positive Feedback: The group forms a circle, and one person will pick another person, stand in front of them, look them in the eye, and tell them what kind of positive changes and growth they have seen in that person since they came to treatment. Once everyone has had a turn, process how they felt giving people compliments, getting compliments, and having to stand there and accept the compliment without saying "No, No."

o I Am: Have the group members think of all the things they enjoy doing in life besides alcohol and drugs. Then ask them to write out every single thing they can think of, starting with "I am." So it may be "I am music; I am laughter; I am a rainy day with raindrops touching my tongue; I am running through the mountains; I am driving down the highway with my window down." Ask for volunteers to share some of what they have written. Ask them what they wrote that was positive.

o Letter to a Teenager: Have group members write a letter to a teenager that they love. It can be a younger brother, sister, niece, or nephew or just somebody they knew in their neighborhood growing up. They should write the letter to the teenager as if they were leaving for college in the next week. The letter should be about what they hope and wish for the teenager during their college experience. They should also include in that letter something about what they hope and wish for in terms of alcohol and drug use during their college years. Then ask them to share their letters if they wish, and discuss how *they* deserve the college experience that they are wishing for this other person that they love, and how they need to treat themselves with this same kind of love and hope for the future as they would have for the teenager.

o <u>Lifeboat:</u> Divide the group into smaller groups and tell them that each group has a lifeboat, but the lifeboat will only fit all but one of them (e.g., if the group is five people, the lifeboat can only hold four). The group members have to talk about why they are valuable and why they should be allowed to get on the boat.

o <u>Mirror Talk:</u> Three times a day for two minutes each, group members are to stand in front of a mirror and say three positive things about themselves. During this time, there is to be no brushing teeth or combing hair or taking care of cosmetic needs. This time is strictly to look in the mirror. When the three positives have been given, the person is to continue looking in the mirror for the full two minutes.

o <u>Nature Association:</u> Ask clients to identify themselves with something in nature (e.g., tree, stream, animal), and then have them describe the importance of that animal and why it is important to the world. Talk about how unique and important each one of those things is to nature and how the clients are also unique and important to human society.

o <u>Self-Inventory:</u> Have group members write down five things they like about themselves and five things they don't like about themselves and process that.

RECOVERY SKILLS: COMMUNICATION/ MINDFULNESS/PROBLEM SOLVING

These exercises are meant to assist clients in developing these recovery skills.

Communication

o <u>"I" Statement Leader Modeling:</u> The leader says to the group, "For the next 30 minutes, I am going to model 'I' statements. If any of you catch me using anything other than 'I' statements, point it out to me, and the first one to point it out to me will get a penny." This exercise (1) models "I" statements for the group; (2) helps members be attentive to what is being said; and (3) holds the leader accountable to the group and therefore models accountability for them.

Mindfulness

o <u>Candy:</u> Have them unwrap a piece of candy, smell the outside of it, feel the texture, pay attention to its sounds, and slowly taste it.

o <u>Guided Imagery:</u> Open group with a guided imagery, such as a meditation, and have everyone work on breathing and feeling where their stress is inside of their bodies.

o <u>Outdoor Items:</u> Bring natural outdoor things into group (e.g., flowers, rocks, petals). Start group by having each person hold one of these natural objects in their hands for a two- or three-minute meditation. Have them concentrate on that object—smelling it, touching it, turning it over, looking at it.

o <u>Outdoor Meditation:</u> Have therapeutic groups end in the serenity prayer in a circle, and take the groups outside and meditate. Tell them, "Don't really look at anything in particular. Allow yourself to see everything at once and be in the moment, because the objective is to look out and notice that you can see movement and things happening."

Problem Solving

o   <u>Monday Writing:</u> Write the word "Monday" on the board in cursive with all the letters connected. Then say, "Is there a way you can write Monday, without connecting the M or the O, and without the pen ever leaving the paper or the board?" The group members will say, "No, that can't be done." However, it can be done. Instead of starting with the letter M, start writing the word "Monday" with the letter O and write "O-N-D-A-Y" and continue the Y to the beginning of the word and add in the M, and the word is written in cursive, without connecting the M and the O.

o   <u>Rock Painting:</u> Bring rocks to group and let members choose the size of their rocks and paint on them the problem they are facing in their recovery. After painting the rocks, they have to hold their rocks until they come up with a reasonable working solution to solve their problems. Process how the rock symbolizes their struggle in recovery.

o   <u>Nine Dots Puzzle:</u> Draw nine dots that form a square (three lines of three dots each). Put a client's name at the top of the square. Ask the client, "How can you make your life come together? If these nine dots represented your life and you had to connect all nine dots with four straight lines, is there a way that you could do that?" Generally, the group members will say that there is no way to do it. However, it can be done by going, literally, outside of the box. Starting at the top left-hand corner, draw a diagonal line to the bottom right-hand corner. Then, draw a line straight up to the top right-hand corner, but then keep going outside the square for a little distance, and come back diagonally to the middle left-hand dot. Keep going outside of the box until you can draw a straight line through the bottom line of dots. By going outside the box you can connect all nine dots. This exercise can be used to demonstrate that things are possible, that sometimes somebody can help show you how to put your life together, and that sometimes you have to think "outside the box."

○ <u>Solution Exploration:</u> Have the group process the issue a client brings up for discussion and let the group come up with the solution.

○ <u>Using Triggers:</u> Have a group member identify a substance abuse trigger, and have them walk the leader through five strategies that they have developed to help them deal with that trigger.

VALUES

These exercises are intended to assist clients in clarifying their values.

○ <u>Airplane/Lifeboat Story:</u> Tell the group a story about a plane that crashes with 12 people on it and that they have a lifeboat, but they can only take six of the 12 crash survivors on the boat. The group has to decide first as individuals and then as a group which six people (each representing a specific value) they will save. After the activity, have each member choose their top five values from a values list and number them 1 (most important) to 5 (least important). Then discuss how their current behaviors align (or don't align) with their values.

○ <u>Drawbridge Exercise:</u> Tell the group the story of a lady who is married to a nobleman. The nobleman leaves the castle and warns the lady that if she leaves, she'll experience a dire consequence. She leaves and visits her lover in the village and upon returning finds a madman at the gate of the drawbridge. The madman warns her that if she tries to cross he will kill her. She goes back to the village to try to get help. She first goes to the lover, who tells her he wants nothing to do with it; she then goes to her best friend, who says she doesn't want anything to do with it because she shouldn't have disobeyed her husband; and then she goes to a boatman, who just wants money. Ultimately, she decides to cross the drawbridge and is killed. The group then tries to determine who is responsible for her death, which elicits a discussion of values and consequences of actions.

- Desert Island Story: Tell a story about a man and a woman who are stranded on a desert island. The man has a disease and has to take medicine every six hours. There is only enough medicine available for one dose. They have one gun and one bullet left. A man in a boat comes to the island and is hungry and has no food. The woman tells the man their situation, and the man says, "If you sleep with me, I will take you back to the United States, but there is only room for two people in my boat." After they hear the story, members are to write down how they would resolve the situation. They are only given three to four minutes. They get into small groups of three or four and have to come to a mutual decision about how to solve the problem. They all have to agree. Process the decisions (how they were made, contributing values) in the group.

- Liver Transplant Scenario: Describe to the group four case histories of people who are on the waiting list for a liver transplant, with the four people pretty evenly matched. Have the group members pretend they're doctors who are on a committee that is going to decide which one of the four people can get the liver. Once the decision is made, the leader receives a phone call from the ICU stating the person they have chosen has died, so now they must choose someone else. Process the values that operated in their decision as well as their reaction to having power over people's lives, as they have in situations such as driving under the influence: at such a time, they have life-and-death power over the people who are out on the highway. The exercise encourages the group to take a look at themselves and the choices they want to make.

o Value Clarification: Have group members write down four things that they value. Then have them remove the thing out of the four that is least valuable to them. Repeat until all of the things are gone. Use this exercise to have group members explore what is important to them and to explore the idea that if they relapse, they may lose these important things.

o What's Important to Me?: Ask the group: "If I was all-powerful and came to you and told you that in 20 minutes you had to move to an unknown destination, and you could pick three things to take with you on this journey (it cannot be a person), what three things would you take with you?" Then process the clients' answers.

OPENERS

Opening Statements

- "Is there anything you need to talk about today?"
- "Any hangover from prior group?"
- "How is everyone doing today?"
- "What do we need to do today?"
- "If everything was perfect in your life, what would your life be like?"
- "How is your family?"
- "I am __; I work at ___."
- "How did we get here?"
- "What do you want to work on today?"
- "How did you get referred?"

General Opening Activities

- Have a welcoming tone.
- Be positive and encouraging.
- Identify a high-risk situation for relapse.
- Discuss accomplishments and challenges ("brags and snags").
- Provide snacks and coffee.
- Identify who is going to be absent.

- Make contact with each person (handshake/speak to them) before group begins or at the beginning of group.
- Ask if anyone has a concern they want to discuss.
- Read daily devotional reading.
- Use humor.
- Introduce a feeling word.
- Ask about goals for that day; fill out form.
- Do a check-in: spiritually, mentally, emotionally, physically.
- Do name introductions and review group norms (e.g., interpersonal safety, confidentiality).
- Discuss sobriety time, talk about what members want to get out of group, and how to treat one another in group.
- Introduce self and opening exercise.
- Summarize previous week's work.
- Have a longer-term member introduce a topic.
- Ask members to take 1 to 3 minutes to get ready/think about what to use group for and how they feel.

Specific Opening Activities

- Write down one thing that you regret in life, put it in a hat, and burn these written regrets at the end of group.
- In weeklong groups, open group on Monday by saying, "Hey, how's everybody doing?" If something sad or good has happened over the weekend, it can be used as the starting point for a conversation.

- Have the clients give a self-assessment of where they think they are in treatment and what they think they're doing.

- Check in and find out how everyone's doing and where they are in terms of their recovery. Also, do a little prayer in recognition for the members we have loved who aren't at group anymore.

- Open a session with current events that we as a community have experienced and/or with a saying or phrase that may have some Zen-like meaning behind it that correlates that with the meaning of life as well as the meaning of new experiences.

- Write an inspirational quote on the board and then have the group discuss it.

- Have members close their eyes and focus on breathing for four breaths. Then they open their eyes and do a check-in. Go around the room and have members tell how they feel about the breathing exercise and coming to the group for treatment. The leader asks members if they have any feedback for other members.

- Have members go around the group and tell how their day has been and how they are feeling. This helps group members focus and relax in order to concentrate on the topic in group. The leader can call them by their first name to make them feel comfortable.

- Break the ice with a simple joke, and then give out information about what's going to be given out in the group in order to try to get the clients' interest.

- Open groups with a daily reading, and pick a topic for that day's group. Pause for effect when picking out what topic to talk about.
- Say "good morning" in an evening group. Then ask clients, "So, what's it going to take for you to wake up in terms of your recovery?" Then say, "If you've got some pressing issue, I want you to think of something that will help you wake up with regard to that issue in your recovery. What is it?"
- Share my (leader) own story with the group—open myself up to help them open up.
- Have group members check in with themselves about where they are spiritually, physically, emotionally, and mentally before group begins.

CLOSERS

Closing Statements

- "Where are you going to go with the input that the group members have given you?"
- "How are you going to remain in recovery 2 more weeks?"
- "What will you do to maintain your sobriety?"
- "Where do we want to go in the next group?"
- "What did you learn from our discussion?"
- "We're done for today."
- "How big is your want to stay sober?"

General Closing Activities

- Give warnings for the time ending.
- Write down one thing you regret in life, put it in a hat, and burn these written regrets at the end of group.
- Ask the clients to share something they heard in group that day that they had never heard before.
- Pick out the positive things that each person has said and close on those positive notes.
- Affirm clients' strengths.
- Make sure everyone feels safe to end group.
- Play music.
- Have people evaluate the group on a scale of 1 to 10 (10 being the best group experience they have ever had).
- Ask everyone to say what they are grateful for and what they need.
- Have everybody say what they are going to do to prepare for relapse before they leave—especially on the last day of group for the week.
- Have each person say one word that they have received from group that day, and have a group hug while closing with the serenity prayer.
- Summarize what went on in group, and then let everybody say in a few words what they liked best about what went on.
- Have each member give another member a compliment before everyone can leave.

- Read an important segment for 15 to 20 minutes from a recovery-related text (e.g., Narcotics Anonymous, Alcoholics Anonymous).
- Have group members make a gratitude list in order to turn their bad days into good days.
- Give out little cards that say, "Good morning, this is your Higher Power; I will be handling all your problems today," and have them put the cards around their homes.
- Give homework between now and next group.
- Say the serenity prayer, do a one-minute relaxation, ask what they are going to work on and what they got out of group.
- Thank people for sharing.
- Summarize the group's work.
- Give a positive affirmation to another group member.
- Have group members place their arms on each others' shoulders in a circle.

Specific Closing Activities

o <u>Amethyst Stones:</u> Give graduates an amethyst stone that they pass around the group, and have each group member tell that person why it was good to have them in group. They each get to touch the stone and then give it back, and that person has to share why the experience was good for them.

○ <u>Certificates:</u> Recognize someone in the group who has done something well—for example, someone who has been honest about a relapse or another difficult situation and has handled it and shared it with the group. Those who have done something noteworthy are presented in group with a certificate with their name on it.

○ <u>Goodbye Group:</u> Ask members who are staying to say goodbye to those leaving and tell something about the people who are leaving: what they like about them, what they learned from them, and what they hope for them.

○ <u>Graduation Ceremony:</u> Have graduates choose a stone with a word like serenity, hope, love, or peace painted on it. People can also get a gold, silver, or bronze certificate, depending on their attendance. When someone chooses a stone, each person in the group takes a turn holding that stone and says something positive about that person, something they have appreciated about that person. The facilitator then says something and distributes the certificates.

○ <u>Group Feedback:</u> Celebrate completion of treatment by asking those people who are completing the treatment program to remain silent for the majority of the group and hear the feedback from others.

Summarize by asking, "How often have you been in a room where you have heard such positive things?" and also ask the completees how often they have heard feedback in a loving and caring way as opposed to being put down.

o **Group Summary:** Have someone who hasn't had the opportunity to say anything in a large group, where not everyone may have the chance to participate and share, to summarize the group experience.

o **Recovery Celebration:** Have a group "birthday recovery" party regularly on a specific day of the week or month (e.g., every third Thursday) where everybody brings food. During the party, celebrate the work that group members have done and how many days they have in recovery. Total up everybody's sober time and get a picture of how much recovery is in that room at that moment. Then make a paper chain and have each client—who hasn't been to a birthday party yet—write down three strengths in their recovery and three things they feel they're struggling with and share them with the group. Then have each client's papers clipped together in a chain and keep the chain in the room to symbolize that they are all connected in their strengths and in their struggles.

4

RESOURCES

This section is a listing of my personal group counseling favorites in terms of readings, workbooks/exercises, icebreaker card exercises, and websites as drawn from my book, *Learning the Language of Addiction Counseling*. These are my personal favorites because I have found them to be pragmatic, useful, succinct, and inviting of group member participation.

READINGS

Kelin, R. H., & Schermer, V. L. (Eds.) (2000). *Group psychotherapy for psychological trauma*. New York, NY: Guilford Press. This book focuses specifically on trauma in terms of group work.

Malekoff, A. (2004). *Group work with adolescents: Principles and practice* (2nd ed.). New York, NY: Guilford Press.

This book has 17 chapters on group work with the adolescent population. Chapter 9 has an appendix that provides information on group manuals specifically designed for this age group.

Rogers, C. (1970). *Carl Rogers on encounter groups.* New York, NY: Perennial.

This book provides an overview of encounter groups.

Substance Abuse and Mental Health Services Administration. (2005). *Substance abuse treatment: Group therapy: Treatment Improvement Protocol (TIP 41) Series* (DHHS Publication No. SMA 05-3991). Rockville, MD: Author.

This book has seven chapters that discuss substance abuse treatment groups in general, types of common groups, placement criteria for clients, group development and tasks, stages of treatment, group leadership, and training/supervision.

White, J. R., & Freeman, A. S. (2000). *Cognitive-behavioral group therapy for specific problems and populations.* Washington, DC: American Psychological Association.

This book provides cognitive-behavioral focus.

Yalom, I. D., & Leszcz, M. (2005).*The theory and practice of group psychotherapy* (5th ed.). New York, NY: Basic Books:

This book provides an in-depth look at group counseling.

WORKBOOKS/EXERCISES

Carrell, S. (2010). *Group exercises for adolescents* (3rd ed.). Thousand Oaks, CA: Sage.

This book provides numerous exercises for working with adolescents.

Connors, G. J., Donovan, D. M., & DiClemente, C. C. (2001). *Substance abuse treatment and the stages of change.* New York, NY: Guilford Press.

This 274-page book has a section on group treatment that discusses "resolution-enhancing" exercises that can assist clients in addressing their ambivalence about their alcohol and drug use (good or less good things about use, decisional balance, looking back/looking forward, exploring goals, the "miracle question").

Corey, G. (2011). *Theory and practice of group counseling* (8th ed.). Belmont, CA: Brooks/Cole.

This 544-page book has five chapters on general group concerns (e.g., leadership, ethics, stages), 11 chapters on specific theoretical approaches to group work (i.e., psychoanalytic, Adlerian, psychodrama, existential, person-centered, Gestalt, transactional analysis, cognitive-behavioral, rational emotive behavior therapy, reality therapy, solution-focused brief therapy), and two chapters on comparing the different theories and looking at group work from an integrated perspective. It has excellent sections in the general group concerns area on proposal development of a group and opening and closing comments for group sessions.

Corey, G., Corey, M. S., Callanan, P., & Russell, J. M. (2004). *Group techniques* (3rd ed.). Pacific Grove, CA: Brooks/Cole.

This 199-page book has two chapters on general and ethical issues related to techniques and five chapters of techniques, each specific to a group stage (i.e., forming, initial, transition, working, final).

DeLucia-Waack, J. L., Bridbord, K. H., Kleiner, J. S., & Nitza, A. G. (2006). *Group work experts share their favorite activities: A guide to choosing, planning, conduction, and processing* (rev. ed.). Alexandria, VA: Association for Specialists in Group Work.

This 189-page workbook has group activities for each stage of group development (i.e., orientation, transition, working, termination).

Dossic, J., & Shea, E. (1988). *Creative therapy: 52 exercises for groups I.* Sarasota, FL: Professional Resource Exchange.

Dossic, J., & Shea, E. (1990). *Creative therapy: 52 exercises for groups II.* Sarasota, FL: Professional Resource Exchange.

Dossic, J., & Shea, E. (1995). *Creative therapy: 52 exercises for groups III.* Sarasota, FL: Professional Resource Exchange.

Each of these books has 52 exercises that are clearly described in terms of how to use them in a group context.

Fleming, M. (1995). *Group activities for adults at risk for chemical dependence.* Minneapolis, MN: Johnson Institute.

This 113-page workbook has numerous exercises that can be used in a group setting for substance-abusing clients.

Greanias, T., & Siegel, S. (2000). Dual diagnosis. In J. R. White & A. S. Freeman (Eds.), *Cognitive-behavioral group therapy for specific problems and populations* (pp. 149–173). Washington, DC: American Psychological Association.

This book chapter provides group assignments for a dual diagnosis group.

Ingersoll, K. S., Wagner, C. C., & Gharib, S. (2002). *Motivational groups for community substance abuse programs*. Richmond, VA: Mid-Atlantic ATTC (804-828-9910) mid-attc@mindspring.com

This book addresses the application of Motivational Interviewing in group therapy with substance abusers.

Metcalf, L. (1998). *Solution focused group therapy.* New York, NY: Free Press.

This book addresses the application of solution-focused therapy in a group setting. It has an excellent admission interview form and forms for notes for the client and therapist to complete after each session to monitor clinical work from a solution-focused perspective.

Mueser, K. T., Noordsy, D. L., Drake, R. E., & Fox, L. (2003). *Integrated treatment for dual disorders.* New York, NY: Guilford Press.

This book has a helpful section (four chapters) on group interventions with persuasion, active treatment, social skills training, and self-help groups when working with dual-disordered clients.

Ragsdale, S., & Saylor, A. (2007). *Great group games.* Minneapolis, MN: Search Institute.

There are 175 exercises formed around the stages of group development that can be used for all ages.

Rohnke, K., & Butler, S. (1995). *Quicksilver.* Dubuque, IA: Kendall/Hunt.

This book consists of activities and adventure games that can be used with groups.

Velasquez, M. M., Maurer, G. G., Crouch, V., & DiClemente, C. C. (2001). *Group treatment for substance abuse: A stages-of-change therapy manual.* New York, NY: Guilford Press.
This 222-page book has three sections: The first section provides an overview of the stages of change model, and the next two sections cover the five stages, providing thorough outlines for each session.

ICEBREAKER EXERCISES

Chat Pack. Available at www.questmarc.com
These cards each have a question on them.
Conversations to Go. Available at www.moonjar.com
These cards come in a box (encouraging people to think outside of the box), and each has a question written on it.
Soul Cards 1 & 2. Available at www.touchdrawing.com
These picture cards can be used to facilitate discussion.
The Feelings Playing Cards. Available at www.timepromotions.com
Each card has a cartoon face and an emotion written on it.

WEBSITES

American Counseling Association

Association for Specialists in Group Work

www.asgw.org

This website provides general information about this division of the American Counseling Association. It also has a variety of resources for counselors, such as videos and a journal. Counselors can join this national division by joining the American Counseling Association.

American Psychological Association

Division 49, Society of Group Psychology and Group Psychotherapy

www.apadivisions.org/division-49/index.aspx

This website is the home page of this division of the American Psychological Association that one can join by joining the APA. It has numerous resources such as publications. Its purpose is to promote group development and the group psychology field through research, teaching, education, and clinical practice.

National Association of Social Workers

www.socialworkers.org

Although this organization does not have a specific division for group work, its website provides numerous group therapy resources for clinicians.

CPSIA inform___
Printed in the
BVOW03n17(

332513E

903957